WALKING ON JURA, ISLAY AND COLONSAY

About the Author

Peter Edwards grew up in Sussex and nurtured a love of walking amid the 'blunt, bow-headed, whale-backed' hills of the South Downs. He has undertaken numerous walking and cycling expeditions in Europe and beyond and is particularly drawn to wild and remote landscapes. After completing his doctorate on British collective memory of the Great War at Sussex University, Peter moved to Scotland in 2006. Peter also writes about his walking and cycling trips on his blog site at www.writesofway.com.

WALKING ON JURA, ISLAY AND COLONSAY

by Peter Edwards

2 POLICE SQUARE, MILNTHORPE, CUMBRIA LA7 7PY
www.cicerone.co.uk

© Peter Edwards 2010
First edition 2010
ISBN: 978 1 85284 610 7

Printed by KHL Printing, Singapore

All photographs are by the author unless otherwise stated.

Acknowledgements

I am grateful to Islay Natural History Trust for permission to use information from their database. I am indebted to Peter Youngson, whose superlative book *Jura: Island of Deer*, has been an invaluable resource. While walking in the Southern Hebrides, I have greatly enjoyed the company of Steve Wilkinson, Dan Twyman, Chris Hallworth, Jon Beck, Sarah Blann and Steve Mason, Garry Glover, Malcolm Walker, Alex Rintoul, Susan Kemp, Felicity Parsons, Anne-Marie and David Parsons and Sol. Thanks to Andy Dodd and Jen Bull for road-testing the prototype. Most of all I would like to thank the lovely Fiona Rintoul who introduced me to these wonderful islands and has been my companion on many fine walks since 2001. This guide is dedicated to her.

Front cover: Near Glendebadel Bay, west coast of Jura

CONTENTS

INTRODUCTION 11
Jura. 12
Islay 13
Colonsay 13
Getting to the Southern Hebrides 14
Getting between the islands 18
The routes. 18
Maps and route finding. 19
Safety and emergencies 20
What to take. 21

JURA 23

Introduction. 25

Walk 1   The west coast walk 43
Day 1   Kinuachdrachd to Glengarrisdale 45
         Alternative: Road End to Glengarrisdale 52
Day 2   Glengarrisdale to Shian Bay 55
Day 3   Shian Bay to Cruib Lodge 61
Day 4   Cruib Lodge to Glenbatrick Bay 71
Day 5   Glenbatrick Bay to Feolin Ferry around the coast 77
         Alternative: Glenbatrick Bay to the A846 via Glen Batrick 83

Walk 2   Walking the Paps of Jura 86

Walk 3   Evans' Walk to Glenbatrick Bay, Feolin Ferry or the head of
         Loch Tarbert 91

ISLAY 101

Introduction 103

Walk 4   Bunnahabhain to Killinallan 116

Walk 5   An Claddach–Beinn Bheigier circuit. 124

Walk 6   The Oa peninsula 133

Walk 7   Sanaigmore to Kilchiaran 142

Walk 8   Ardnave to Sanaigmore. 148

COLONSAY 151

Introduction 153

Walk 9   South Colonsay coast and Oronsay 164

Walk 10   Lower Kilchattan to Kiloran Bay 173

Walk 11   Kiloran Bay to Scalasaig around the coast 179

Walk 12   Scalasaig to Kiloran Bay along the Old Road 185

APPENDIX A   Accommodation 189
APPENDIX B   Other useful contacts 195
APPENDIX C   Glossary 197
APPENDIX D   Further reading 198

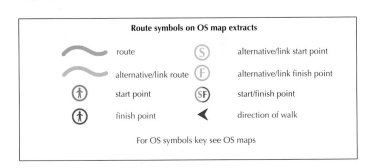

Route symbols on OS map extracts

route	S alternative/link start point
alternative/link route	F alternative/link finish point
start point	SF start/finish point
finish point	◄ direction of walk

For OS symbols key see OS maps

Negotiating the rocky coastline at Aird Bhreacain

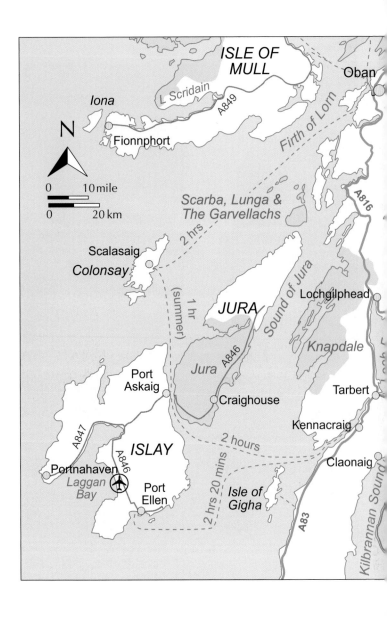

Driftwood fire at Shian Bay

INTRODUCTION

The south shore of Loch Tarbert (Walk 1, Day 4)

Tucked away off the Kintyre peninsula 80km (50 miles) or so west of Glasgow as the crow flies, the Southern Hebrides are often overlooked by walkers and other visitors magnetically attracted by the grandeur of the Highlands and the Isle of Skye further north. But Jura, Islay and Colonsay are no less beautiful than those illustrious regions, although their charms are perhaps more understated.

The wild and beautiful Southern Hebrides provide a magnificent setting for some of the finest and most challenging walking to be found in Scotland, or indeed anywhere in the British Isles. The islands' sublime coastal landscapes of rugged quartzite rock, white sandy bays and sparkling turquoise waters teem with wildlife and a profusion of breathtaking geological phenomena.

A real sense of remoteness is found among the hills and along the shores of these wonderful islands, not least because you are more likely to share the landscape with eagles, otters, seals, wild goats and red deer than with other people. For those who like to get away from the madding crowd and enjoy the peace and serenity of walking amid landscapes untrammelled by the depredations of mass tourism, these islands are a natural sanctuary. Furthermore, the tourism infrastructure on the islands, which is refreshingly low-key on Jura and Colonsay in particular, is characterised by quality and value for money.

JURA

The west coast of Jura is as pristine an area of natural wilderness as can be found anywhere in western Europe. It is uninhabited by humans, there is no livestock grazing, very little land management and the only buildings along the 80km (50 miles) shoreline between Kinuachdrachd in the north and Feolin Ferry in the south are the bothies at Glengarrisdale, Ruantallain and Cruib Lodge and the summer house at Glenbatrick Bay. The great natural beauty of the west coast, with its quartzite rock, emerald and whisky-hued hills, white sands and turquoise waters, is enhanced by its profusion of remarkable geological phenomena and abundant wildlife. Furthermore, few places in the British Isles combine such multifaceted splendour with the possibility of complete solitude. In the autumn, spring and winter months it is possible to walk on the west coast for days without encountering anyone else at all.

One reason for the dearth of visitors to this wonderful place lies in its remoteness. It takes a certain amount of planning and a degree of application to arrive at the start of the west coast walk – wherever you decide that the start is. George Orwell, that best-known temporary *Diurach* (inhabitant of Jura), famously described his retreat at Barnhill – 1.5km south of Kinuachdrachd – as 'ungetatable'.

Another reason is that walking the route is a challenging enterprise. When walking the west coast of Jura was first proposed to me some years ago, I set about finding a guidebook. The search turned up any number of books guiding the theoretical walker over the famous Paps of Jura and on other less challenging routes. When it came to the island's west coast, however, I encountered an empty

The Paps of Jura

void into which a handful of adjectives – 'remote', 'wild', 'untamed', 'forbidding' – had been scattered. This absence made the prospect all the more compelling and my first visit to north-western Jura left me feeling that I'd been let in on a fantastic secret. You might ask why I want to advertise this secret when it was the silence on the subject that so appealed in the first place. I believe the west coast of Jura is one of the truly great walks in the British Isles and deserves its place in the canon. Its remoteness and the challenging nature of the walk mean it is never likely to become oversubscribed.

Among the other walks on Jura described in this book is a round of the island's trio of distinctive quartzite peaks. The Paps may not be Munros – at 785m Beinn an Oir is a Corbett – but they rise from sea level and a round of all three mountains involves some 1500m of ascent and is a hillwalking classic. A detailed route description helps walkers make the best of a tough day on testing terrain. Several other day walks on the island provide challenging routes, although on a slightly less epic scale.

and remote clifftops are accessible by road. The walks described here are as grand in scale as those on Jura. They include the rugged coastline and magnificent bays of the Atlantic coast, the dramatic cliffs of the Oa peninsula and the spectacular route from Bunnahabhain on the Sound of Islay to Kilinallan on Loch Gruinart.

Islay has an abundance of wildlife and is particularly famous for its spectacular birdlife, including the huge numbers of migratory geese that arrive each October. The landscape is awash with history; the coastline is ringed with Iron Age hill forts and garlanded with infamous shipwrecks, while the hinterland is dotted with the remains of settlements, both ancient and more recent – including the mediaeval seat of the Lords of the Isles at Finlaggan.

Islay also offers the tired walker all the comforts of civilisation in a beautiful setting. There are many good places to eat, including some excellent pubs, a range of great places to stay, including two beautifully situated campsites and an excellent youth hostel, and eight whisky distilleries.

ISLAY

Islay is lower lying, more populous and more developed than its rugged neighbour; however, it has many kilometres of varied and beautiful coastline and, unlike Jura, walks along some of the island's deserted shores

COLONSAY

Colonsay is a small but perfectly formed gem of an island, which distils much of the natural splendour of its neighbours into a relatively compact area. Much more than a facsimile of Jura and Islay in miniature, it is an island with a very distinct character of

13

Oronsay

its own, epitomised by its innate tranquillity. The walks described here take in some remarkably varied terrain, from high cliffs to vast white sandy bays, amid some of the most sublime coastal landscapes found anywhere in the British Isles.

From any point on Colonsay, wild and beautiful landscapes are only a short walk away. A kilometre from the settlement of Lower Kilchattan, vast colonies of seabirds nest on the vertiginous cliffs of the west coast. A walk around the south coast, including Colonsay's tide-separated sister island of Oronsay, takes in some wonderful beach and dune-fringed shoreline, with fine views of Jura and Islay across the Firth of Lorn. A walk around the rugged north of the island is more of a challenge, but visits beautiful landscape full of interest, including the superlative sandy bays of Kiloran and Balnahard. Somewhat surprisingly,

given Colonsay's size, few other people are encountered once the island's few kilometres of road are left behind. The island's compact nature also means walks can be adapted to almost any length.

GETTING TO THE SOUTHERN HEBRIDES

Jura
The most frequented route to Jura is via Islay but it is possible to get there direct from the mainland.

Jura by water taxi
Duncan Philips operates Farsain Cruises out of Craobh Haven Marina, north of Lochgilphead on the Kintyre coast. The crossing to Kinuachdrachd takes an hour and at the time of writing (2009) costs £70 one-way regardless of the size of the group. If travelling in a group to walk the west

The MV Hebridean Isles at Port Askaig on the Sound of Islay

coast of Jura, it saves time and makes economic sense to take the Glasgow–Campbeltown bus to Lochgilphead, a taxi from there to Craobh Haven, then go on to Kinuachdrachd by water taxi. This way you can leave Glasgow at 9am and arrive at Kinuachdrachd as early as 1pm, allowing an afternoon's walk and cutting out the 15km (9 mile) yomp from Ardlussa (see below). Contact Farsain Cruises on 01852 500664 or 07880 714165. For the Lochgilphead–Croabh Haven leg, contact John Byrne of Glenfyne Taxis on 07850 645671. John uses a 'people carrier' with a roof box for groups of up to six with rucksacks. Gemini Cruises also operates a water taxi between Crinan Harbour and Jura, www.gemini-crinan.co.uk.

Tayvallich–Craighouse Ferry
The summer ferry service between Tayvallich on the Kintyre peninsula and Craighouse has operated since 2008. The ferry is a rigid inflatable boat (RIB) and carries 15 passengers, making the crossing in under an hour. The service runs several times a day, subject to conditions, and operates between late April and the end of September. Advance reservations should be made. For timetables and reservations contact 07768 450000.

Islay
Caledonian MacBrayne (also known as CalMac) operates the ferry services between Kennacraig and Islay. Ferries from Kennacraig arrive either in Port Askaig or Port Ellen. The crossing takes 2hrs to Port Askaig and 2hrs 20mins to Port Ellen. In summer there are four crossings a day, three on Wednesdays and Sundays. In winter the service is reduced. Check the Caledonian MacBrayne website – www.calmac.co.uk – for timetables or

15

The Sound of Islay

call the port office at Kennacraig on 01880 730253.

From Port Ellen, there is a connecting bus service to port Askaig (451 or 456), which takes 50mins. You may need to change buses at Bowmore. The 1830 Jura Ferry will await the 1745 bus from Port Ellen, scheduled to arrive at 1835, if requested in advance on 01496 840681.

Glasgow to Kennacraig by car

Although Jura lies only 80km (50 miles) from Glasgow as the crow flies, the distance by road to Kennacraig is about 145km (90 miles). This leg of the journey should take 2½–3hrs. Take the A82 from Glasgow (or from the Erskine Bridge, if bypassing Glasgow on the M8) as far as Tarbet, Loch Lomond, then take the A83 in the direction of Campbeltown. The

Kennacraig ferry terminal is 7km beyond Tarbert, Loch Fyne.

Glasgow to Kennacraig by bus

Following the route described above, West Coast Motors www.westcoast motors.co.uk and Scottish Citylink www.citylink.co.uk operate bus services between Glasgow Buchanan Street Bus Station and Campbeltown that connect with the ferry at Kennacraig. For schedule information, contact the Travel Centre at Buchanan Street Bus Station on 041 332 7133.

Glasgow to Islay by air

British Airways runs a twice-daily scheduled service from Glasgow Airport to Islay, which takes 35mins. This service is operated by Loganair. For information on schedules, contact British Airways at Glasgow Airport on

0141 887 1111 or Islay Airport on 01496 302022. To make bookings call 0870 850 9850. Visit www.ba.com for timetables and online booking. A bus service operates between Islay Airport, Bowmore and Port Askaig.

Colonsay

The Caledonian MacBrayne ferry service from Oban to Scalasaig runs five times weekly in summer and three times in the winter. The crossing takes 2hrs 15mins each way and there are great views of the isles of Kerrera, Mull, Seil, Luing, Scarba, the Garvellachs and the west coast of Jura. If you're lucky you may see dolphins, porpoises, minke whales or basking sharks. There is also a return service from Kennacraig to Oban via Port Askaig and Colonsay on Wednesdays only between the beginning of April and the end of October (check the CalMac timetables at www.calmac.co.uk or call 01475 650100 for up-to-date information). (For travel to Kennacraig from Glasgow, see section for Jura.) This service is ideal for making a day trip from Islay, leaving Port Askaig at 1015 and arriving back at 1915, giving visitors 6½ hrs on Colonsay.

Glasgow to Oban by train

There is a connecting train service from Glasgow to Oban on Mondays, Wednesdays, Fridays and Sundays. There are connecting trains to Glasgow from Oban for the ferry arriving from Scalasaig on Tuesdays, Wednesdays and Thursdays only.

Glasgow to Oban by bus

Scottish Citylink Coaches operates an extensive bus service between

Colonsay's wild east coast is a jungle in summer

Glasgow and Oban that takes around 3hrs. The possible permutations are endless, but you should be able to find a service that arrives or departs Oban to connect with your ferry, though you may have to wait for a couple of hours. Consult the relevant timetables at www.citylink.co.uk or contact the Travel Centre at Buchanan Street Bus Station on 0141 332 7133.

Glasgow to Oban by road
Take the A82 from Glasgow (or the Erskine Bridge, if bypassing Glasgow on the M8) towards Loch Lomond and the Trossachs National Park. Keep to the A82 along the western shore of Loch Lomond and on through Crianlarich to Tyndrum. At Tyndrum head west along the A85, passing through Dalmally then along the north shore of Loch Awe, through Taynuilt and along the south shore of Loch Etive before arriving at Oban in around 2½–3hrs. An alternative route, which is arguably more scenic and takes roughly the same time, follows the route from Glasgow as far as Tarbet, Loch Lomond, then takes the A83 in the direction of Campbeltown. From Inverary take the A819 north for about 22km before intersecting with the A85 at the north-eastern tip of Loch Awe and continuing to Oban as above.

Flying to Colonsay from Oban
Highland Airways operates a year-round, twice-daily service between Oban and Colonsay on Tuesdays and Thursdays. Flights depart Oban at

0830 and 1700 (1500 in winter) and take 25mins. Flights depart Colonsay at 0910 and 1740 (1540 in winter). Costs vary, but if booked in advance fares can be as low as £60 return. The flight takes in some magnificent scenery – reason enough to justify the expense. Tickets can be booked online at www.highlandairways.co.uk or by phoning 0845 450 2245.

GETTING BETWEEN THE ISLANDS

The Islay–Jura ferry sails from Port Askaig across the Sound of Islay to Feolin Ferry on the south-west of Jura. The crossing is less than 1km and takes 5mins. The ferry runs at approximately 30min intervals daily from 0730, with the last crossing from Islay to Jura at 1830, returning at 1840. There is a 1930 crossing, returning at 1940, on Wednesdays only. Advance booking is not required. The last crossing from Feolin in advance of the 1530 ferry from Port Askaig to Kennacraig is at 1425 on weekdays and Saturdays and at 1410 on Sundays. The tariff is £2.50 return for foot passengers and £15 per car and driver. Schedules can be checked and bookings made on 01496 840681.

THE ROUTES

This guidebook provides detailed descriptions of 12 challenging coastal and hill walks on the often rugged, but sublimely beautiful islands of the

Southern Hebrides. Many of the walks have not appeared in any previous guide, including the book's centre-piece – the epic five-day route around the west coast of Jura.

These are mostly demanding routes suitable only for fit, competent and well-equipped walkers. The terrain is extremely varied and often challenging, and almost entirely without waymarks or established footpaths. However, the rewards for the adventurous walker are manifold. The routes included in this guide traverse some breathtakingly beautiful scenery full of historical interest and are alive with a profusion of plants and wildlife.

MAPS AND ROUTE FINDING

It is essential that you are equipped with the appropriate maps for under-taking the walks described in this guide. There are almost no waymarks, signposts or even paths of any kind on the routes covered here, mak-ing accurate route finding all the more important. Even walking on the coastal routes is far from straightfor-ward as there are many impassable sections where the shoreline has to be abandoned for higher ground or other natural features need to be negotiated. This guide incorporates Ordnance Survey 1:50,000 mapping with high-lighted routes. These should be used in conjunction with OS Explorer 1:25,000 maps because of the greater topographic detail they afford. Do not rely solely on the maps in this guide-book as it is essential that you can ascertain your position in the wider context, should you need to abandon your walk and make for the nearest road or habitation.

Wild goat and deer tracks can be useful for negotiating the often challenging terrain – especially on

Wild goats near Shian Bay

Jura and Islay (there are no deer on Colonsay), but these should be followed with a degree of caution.

The walks described in this guide are covered by the following Ordnance Survey maps:

• OS Explorer 1:25,000 sheet 355 Jura and Scarba
• OS Explorer 1:25,000 sheet 353 Islay North
• OS Explorer 1:25,000 sheet 352 Islay South
• OS Explorer 1:25,000 sheet 354 Colonsay and Oronsay
• OS Landranger 1:50,000 sheet 60 Islay
• OS Landranger 1:50,000 sheet 61 Jura and Colonsay

SAFETY AND EMERGENCIES

In fine weather the Southern Hebrides can seem like an earthly paradise. However, the onset of high winds and driving rain can rapidly make the place feel quite hellish, especially if you are exposed to the elements. It is therefore very important that you are properly equipped (see below) and are able to navigate proficiently in poor visibility. Check the weather forecast before embarking on your walks and allow yourself plenty of time to complete your day's itinerary. Be aware of the available daylight hours. Always let someone know your intended route and estimated time of completion. Carry a medical kit, survival blanket, mobile phone and plenty of food.

Wear at least one item of high-visibility clothing. A whistle and/or torch are important for attracting attention in case of injury. Six blasts on the whistle or six torch flashes should be repeated every minute.

In case of injury or other incident, try to stay calm and assess your situation. If anyone is injured remember ABC – airway, breathing, circulation (signs of life, blood loss). Make any casualties warm and comfortable and place any unconscious casualties in the recovery position. Try to ascertain your exact position on the map and consider your options for walking to safety, finding shelter, staying put or seeking help. (Remember that it may take an emergency team some hours to reach you, especially in poor conditions in a remote area.)

If you decide to call for help, phone 999 and ask for the Police and Mountain Rescue. Be ready to give the location of the incident (grid references, map sheet number, name of the area and description of the terrain), number and names of people in the party and their condition, any injuries and names of casualties. Be prepared to supply the numbers of any phones carried by the party; describe the nature and time of the incident, weather conditions, including wind speed and visibility at the incident site, equipment at the site, including warm clothing and shelter, distinguishing features and markers at the site, and the location from which you are phoning if different from the incident site.

Most of the walks described here are very challenging and it is best not to attempt the majority of them on your own. Likewise, these walks should only be undertaken by fit and experienced walkers and are not suitable for the very elderly, very young or anyone carrying an injury.

WHAT TO TAKE

As mentioned above, the OS Explorer 1:25,000 maps are indispensable, as is a compass. Using a waterproof map case is advisable. A 'wristwatch' altimeter is also useful for navigation, especially in the hills. It's not quite so easy to get lost when walking along the coast, but it is always worth knowing exactly where you are, especially in poor weather and low visibility. Furthermore, being able to navigate

proficiently is essential if for any reason you need to head inland from the coast.

A robust rucksack with adequate capacity and a comfortable harness is indispensable, as is a waterproof pack liner. For day walks, a 30+ litre pack should be sufficient; for longer trips, when you are carrying camping gear and several days' food, a 60+ litre pack may be required. Effective waterproofs are always essential when undertaking a walk of any length in the Southern Hebrides. Weather can change quickly on the islands and doesn't always obey the forecasts. Lightweight, 'wickable', quick-drying clothing is also a must when walking the often strenuous routes described in this guide. Be sure to have adequate warm clothing; extra layers are useful for when you take breaks. The nature

Summer twilight at Shian Bay

of the terrain also requires that you wear robust walking boots with ankle support and a Vibram sole. It is difficult to keep your feet dry at the best of times when walking on the islands, so non-leaky, Gore-Tex-lined or well-waxed boots are essential. Gaiters are also indispensable on terrain that can be very boggy in places. Telescopic walking poles are also very useful for the challenging terrain encountered on the walks described here, especially when carrying a heavy pack. With the possible exception of mid-summer, a warm hat and gloves should find a place in your rucksack. Sun cream, a sun hat and sunglasses should also be carried from spring through to autumn.

Always carry plenty of food, including high-energy snacks and some water. (There are usually frequent opportunities to fill up from the islands' numerous burns. The water is generally safe to drink and tastes wonderful; however, iodine or other water-purifying tablets can be carried if you are worried about contamination.) A basic medical kit and a survival bag should always be carried and a mobile phone is also useful in case of misadventure. A head torch is invaluable if you are benighted and can help to attract attention in an emergency; carrying a whistle is useful for the same purpose. From late spring until late autumn it is worth carrying some serious insect repellent, and a midge/mosquito hat. In addition to its other uses, a Swiss army knife with tweezers is handy for tick-removal. Lightweight binoculars are worth their weight for admiring the islands' splendid wildlife.

JURA

Waterfall at Sliabh allt an Tairbh (Walk 1, Day 2)

23

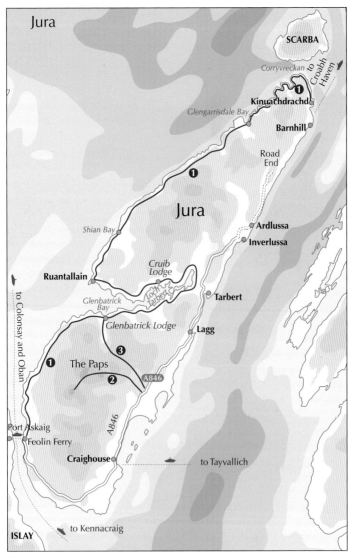

INTRODUCTION

Glendebadel Bay (Walk 1, Day 2)

The wildest of the Southern Hebrides, Jura lies some 80km (50 miles) west of Glasgow as the crow flies and is separated from the mainland by the Sound of Jura – just a few miles wide at its narrowest point. The island is approximately 50km (30 miles) in length and 13km (9 miles) across at its widest point. The north and south parts are almost completely bisected by Loch Tarbert, a 1km-wide isthmus separating the sea loch from the Sound of Jura. The island's most famous and striking physical features are the Paps of Jura – three breast-shaped, quartzite scree-clad mountains each rising in excess of 730m (2400ft) above sea level.

To the south-west of Jura, less than 1km across the Sound of Islay, lies the isle of Islay – Jura's larger and more populous neighbour. Their proximity belies the marked physical differences between them. Islay has a generally softer countenance with tracts of low-lying cultivated land, the sky-reflecting expanse of Loch Indaal and a scattering of sizeable settlements with characteristic white-washed houses. Fifteen kilometres to the west, across the Firth of Lorn, lies the small and perfectly formed isle of Colonsay and its sister island Oronsay.

Jura is often described as the most rugged of the Southern Hebrides and this description is true of all but the most sheltered areas along the island's east coast. The interior is mountainous and boggy, making the island largely unsuited to cultivation. This is the chief reason for Jura's small population, which has hovered below the 200 mark in recent years. This statistic makes Jura the least-populated area of Europe, a thought-provoking detail when one considers that the Ural Mountains form Europe's eastern boundary. Most of the population is centred around the island's 'capital', Craighouse, with other settlements strung along the east coast at Ardfin, Knockrome, Lagg, Tarbert and Inverlussa. Today, much of the working population is employed in the management of the island's eight estates, including deer stalking and fisheries, with the Isle of Jura whisky distillery, crofting, tourism, and inshore fishing accounting for much of the rest.

HISTORY

All traces of Palaeolithic (Old Stone Age) settlement in Scotland were obliterated by the ice sheets during the Quarternary glaciation. However, a great deal of light was cast on the subsequent prehistory of Jura by the late John Mercer, a palaeontologist who lived on the island between the 1960s and 1980s. Mercer's archaeological investigations unearthed evidence of Mesolithic settlement from around 7000BC, with hunter-gatherers in seasonal occupation as early as 10,500BC on the fringes of the retreating ice sheet.

Mercer identified Mesolithic camps on the east coast, north of Tarbert, at Lussa River, Lealt and An Carn and at Glenbatrick on the west coast.

Few traces of the Neolithic Age have been discovered on Jura, with no known settlements dating from the period (4000–2000BC). The sole identified Neolithic site is the chambered cairn at Poll a' Cheo near the island's southern tip (NR504631). Evidence of Bronze Age settlement is more plentiful with a number of cairn and cist burial sites, cup-marked rocks, standing stones and hut circles, including the site at Cul a' Bhaile (NR549726) near Knockrome with its associated field enclosure. Compared with Islay and Colonsay, there are few remains of Iron Age (600BC–AD400) structures on Jura. These amount to five forts and six duns – smaller fortified structures. Compared with the lower-lying and more fertile neighbouring islands, the rugged, boggy terrain of Jura was always less viable for settlement.

From the early part of the third century an Irish tribe – Scotti of Dál Riata, led by Cairbre Riata – began the colonisation of the Kintyre peninsula and the Inner Hebrides. Cairbre Riata's descendants, Fergus, Loarn and Angus, continued the process of conquering and colonisation and the decisive invasion of Argyll took place late in the fifth century. Angus took possession of Islay and Jura.

In AD563 St Columba and his followers arrived in the Inner Hebrides

*Beinn an Oir and Beinn Shiantaidh
from Beinn a' Chaolais (Walk 2)*

from Ireland. Columba is said to have landed on Oronsay before voyaging on to Iona where he established what would become the important ecclesiastical centre of Iona Abbey. The Celtic Christian missionaries set about converting the populations of the islands and the mainland. St Columba's uncle, St Ernan, has been linked to Jura, which is thought to be the location of the lost Christian community of Hinba.

In AD794, Iona suffered the first of many Viking raids, which gradually forced the monastery into decline. In common with the other islands of the Hebrides, Jura soon came under the Norse sphere of influence. Although there is no evidence of Viking raids or settlements on Jura, oral tradition tells of 'lost battles' at Inver and Ardfin. The island has many Norse place names, such as Liundale, Sannaig and Rainberg Mor.

The Lords of the Isles

The Norsemen ruled the islands from the Isle of Man until Somerled divided the Norse Kingdom of Man and the Isles by defeating Godred's forces in a sea battle off the west coast of Islay in 1156. Somerled's descendants, Clan Donald – known as the Lords of the Isles, extended their sphere of influence to the entire west coast and parts of northern Scotland, which they ruled from Finlaggan on Islay. The MacDonalds controlled Jura until the 1490s, through the agency of the Macleans, Buies and Darrochs. However, the Lordship came to an end after John MacDonald II signed a secret treaty with Edward IV of England against the Scottish Crown, hoping to become King of Scotland in return for his allegiance. Instead, his duplicity led to the forfeiture of all MacDonald land and power on Jura. The island was then bestowed on a branch of the House of Campbell at the Treaty of Camus an Staca in 1506.

The Macleans sought to take advantage of the decline of their former masters, the MacDonalds, and from their base at Aros Castle in Glen Garrisdale they strove to keep the Campbells out of north Jura – finally selling their holdings to Donald McNeil of Colonsay in 1737. Nonetheless, the early 1600s marked the beginning of a long period of Clan Campbell control on Jura, during which 11 successive Campbell lairds ruled the island.

Population decline
The ascendancy of the Campbells marked the beginning of population decline on Jura. Many islanders moved north with the MacDonalds and others were forcibly removed to the Borders region by the Scottish Crown. By the early years of the 18th century many islanders, suffering food shortages, oppressive landowners and the implications of land use change, set sail for the New World. Islanders emigrated to North Carolina, Georgia, Virginia and eastern Canada.

By the late 1700s, the combined forces of industrialisation, the market economy and increased militarisation had given rise to a huge demand for wool for uniforms. Throughout the Highlands and Islands populations were 'cleared' from the land by unscrupulous landowners keen to cash in on the ovine gold rush. The Campbells and McNeil of Colonsay

were no exception. However, no actual 'clearance' took place on Jura; rather the Campbells employed more insidious methods, increasing rents and workloads on their tenants. The establishment of the Jura 'deer forest' for the lucrative 'sporting' market in the late 1860s resulted in further loss of crofting land.

Like many British landowning families, the Campbells suffered as a result of the Great War and the social and economic changes of its aftermath. The Campbell's lost two sons in the war and Charles Campbell returned from the front to inherit an estate in straitened circumstances. By 1938 he had sold the last remnants of the Jura Estate and Jura House.

George Orwell
In the wake of the Second World War the agrarian economy of the island fluctuated and the population continued to decline. In May 1946, amid the post-war world of austerity and rationing, George Orwell came to live at Barnhill near Jura's north-eastern tip and began writing *Nineteen Eighty-Four*, his bleak imagining of a totalitarian dystopia of the near-future. He was soon joined by his infant son Richard, his sister Avril and a young housekeeper. Orwell had wanted to get away from the distractions of London to write what was provisionally entitled *The Last Man in Europe*, but he was also drawn to the notion of self-sufficiency. With the help of Bill Dunn, a young Scot who had lost a

leg in the war, Orwell turned his hand to running a smallholding at Barnhill, though with limited success.

It seems that the *Diurachs* regarded Eric Blair – as they knew him – as 'a kindly and peculiar gentleman' and his biographer, Sir Bernard Crick, believes that Orwell would have stayed on Jura had his health not determined otherwise.

In December 1947, Orwell was diagnosed with tuberculosis and was admitted to hospital near Glasgow. He was able to return to Jura the following July, and in December 1948 he submitted the finished typescript to his publishers. The following month, in very poor health, he left Jura for a sanatorium in Gloucestershire. He died on 21 January 1950, six months after *Nineteen Eighty-Four* was published to instant critical and popular acclaim.

The post-war years of austerity and continuing depopulation presaged a period of stagnation on Jura. However, the island's economic situation has recently begun to improve and the process of population decline has been thrown in to reverse as initiatives to encourage incomers to settle and young *Diurachs* to stay or return have had some success.

GEOLOGY

Excepting the low-lying areas of the east coast, which mainly consist of Scarba conglomerate and Port Ellen phyllites, the Isle of Jura is largely formed of Jura quartzite, a metamorphic rock which has its origins in the late Pre-Cambrian or Dalradian age. The predomination of quartzite is most apparent amid the Paps and the ridges in the island's north-west.

A series of linear basalt dikes cut into the quartzite rock on a southeast–north-west orientation throughout the island, although they are more

Basalt dike near Sliabh allt an Tairbh (Walk 1, Day 2)

Massive raised beach near Ruantallain

numerous in the south. They were formed during a period of intense volcanic activity in the Lower Tertiary period, some 56 million years ago, when upwelling magma filled cracks in the Earth's crust radiating out from centres of eruption on Arran and Mull. Today, these dikes are most apparent on the west coast where erosion of the less-resistant rock into which they are intruded has left them exposed as natural walls.

Jura is internationally renowned for its raised shore platforms and immense raised beaches, which abound on the west coast along with numerous caves, rock stacks and rock arches. These geological phenomena reflect changes in relative sea level associated with the advance and retreat of ice sheets during the Quaternary Ice Age. During glacial periods, sea levels dropped as fresh waters were held captive by the

advancing ice sheets, and rose again when the glaciers melted. At the same time, the landmass initially sank under the weight of the ice cap then gradually rose again as the ice retreated in a process geologists describe as 'glacio-isostatic uplift'. The land rebounded more slowly than the sea level rose, therefore the sea level was initially much higher locally than it is today and beaches and shore platforms were gradually lifted out of the sea as the land continued to rise. The relative rebound is greater in those areas where the ice sheet was thickest and this is why the uplift is more pronounced towards the north-west end of Jura.

The raised beaches along the west coast are impressively proportioned, occurring as terraces or 'staircases' of largely unvegetated shingle ridges, which evidence the gradual fall in relative sea level. The most impressive raised beaches lie between Shian Bay and Ruantallain, east of Ruantallain, west of Glenbatrick above Loch Tarbert, with perhaps the most remarkable formation being the massive pebble bank east of Glenbatrick, which forms a natural barrier between Loch Tarbert and the freshwater Lochan Maol an t-Sornaich. Raised beaches do occur on the sheltered east coast, though these are most often covered in vegetation. The absence of vegetation on the west coast's raised beaches makes these often huge tracts of large cobbles visually spectacular. The size of the cobbles and the depth of deposits, combined with the scouring effects of wind and rain, have rendered these beaches largely sterile.

Jura is also home to an excellently preserved medial moraine known as Sgriob na Caillich (the old woman's slide), which extends for 3km (2 miles) westwards towards the coast from the flank of Beinn an Oir – the highest of the Paps. The moraine takes the form of a series of parallel belts of boulders and is best viewed from across the Sound of Islay. It was formed by the retreat of the Late Devensian ice sheet and is regarded as the best example of its kind in Britain.

WILDLIFE

Jura is renowned for its large population of red deer, which is kept to around 6000 by the estates' gamekeepers and their paying guests during the stalking season (1 July to 20 October for stags and from 21 October to 15 February for hinds). Red deer have long been synonymous with the island. Dhiura, the Gaelic name for the island, derives from the Norse *Dyr ey* or *Diera*, meaning 'deer island'. The deer population grew exponentially with the expansion of the Jura 'deer forest' for commercial sport

Young feral goats

31

in the latter half of the 19th century. They graze on the lower ground during the winter and take to the higher ground during the summer months as the grazing improves there. The mating season or 'rut' takes place during late September and October, when the stags engage in antlered combat for their own harem of hinds and the hills are alive with the sound of their throaty barking. Jura is known for a unique variant among its red deer stags – 'Cromies' get their name from the Gaelic for 'crooked' and have antlers that are distinctively swept back.

Wild goats are found in upland and coastal areas of Scotland and Jura has a population of around 500. Legend has it that they are descended from animals that made it ashore when ships from the Spanish Armada were wrecked nearby. However, they are probably descended from domestic animals kept by crofters and abandoned during the social changes of the mid-19th century. Jura's wild goats are usually dark brown with white patches or entirely dark brown. They have long, shaggy coats and the billy goats have curving, swept-back horns. They are frequently encountered on the north-west coast where small tribes can be found grazing on seaweed along the shore. They are shy beasts and will skitter away when disturbed. Kids are born from late January and are unfeasibly cute.

Atlantic grey and common seals are abundant around Jura and are frequently seen basking on offshore rocks or observing onshore activity from the sea. Around 40 per cent of the world population of grey seals is found around Britain's shores, with 90 per cent of those breeding in Scotland. In the autumn, female grey seals come ashore to give birth to a single white-coated pup, which is left to fend for itself after three weeks. There are small colonies around the north-west of Loch Tarbert.

Otters are well established on Jura and are now protected from persecution. They are found all around Jura's 185km coastline and breeding pairs usually have a coastal territory of around 5km (3 miles) in length. The chances of seeing an otter when walking on Jura's coast are quite good. They are most often seen when hunting just off shore.

Rabbits are plentiful on Jura, though their population is subject to myxomatosis. The mountain hare was introduced to the island around 1900 and has thrived. Stoats are regarded as vermin and are controlled by gamekeepers, though they are still common. The sub-species found here – *Mustela erminea ricinae* – is endemic to Jura and Islay. The brown rat, field vole, wood mouse, house mouse, common shrew and pygmy shrew are also found on Jura, as are the pipistrelle and long-eared bat.

Three amphibians are found on Jura; frogs, toads and palmate newts are all plentiful and three reptiles – the

Oystercatcher eggs at Shian Bay (Walk 1, Day 2)

slow worm, common lizard and adder are also found on the island.

There are robust populations of various raptors resident on Jura, including merlins, kestrels, sparrowhawks, hen harriers, peregrines, buzzards, golden eagles, tawny owls, short-eared owls and barn owls. A pair of sea eagles has recently taken up residence at the north of the island and there's a good chance of spotting one when in the environs of Kinuachdrachd and the Gulf of Corryvreckan. The rare chough is present and ravens are relatively common. Divers, shags, guillemots, gannets and auks are all seen around the coast, as are gulls and waders such as curlews and oyster catchers. Geese and ducks are less frequent here than on Islay,

where huge numbers of migratory geese arrive during the autumn.

Common dolphins are occasionally seen off Jura's shores and, less frequently, other varieties of dolphin, porpoise and whale.

PLANTS AND FLOWERS
Several factors influence the nature and distribution of vegetation on Jura. The long days and high rainfall during the summer months, allied to the temperate influence of the Gulf Stream in winter, promote rapid growth. However, the west coast and areas of high ground are exposed to high winds, which prevent many species gaining a foothold. The underlying geology is also a key factor, with quartzite and other acidic rocks

33

predominating. The combination of high acidity, low mean temperatures and high precipitation means that large areas of the island's soil layer consist of peat.

This results in a contrast between the eastern and western sides of the island. There are palm trees growing at Craighouse on the east coast and at nearby Jura House on the Ardfin estate there is a large collection of ornamental and non-hardy plants, including an Australasian collection, that would struggle to establish themselves in less clement conditions even significantly further south.

The small remnants of native woodland and non-native plantations are also predominantly located on the east of the island, with the exception of native birch woods in Glen Trosdale in the island's far north and at Coille na h'Uanair near Inver on the Sound of Islay. The best native woodland remnants are in the environs of Kinuachdrachd in the far north-east and the fragment of oak-wood above Tramaig Bay, north of Ardlussa.

From 1951, the Forestry Commission acquired around 2000 acres of land and began planting at Sannaig at the island's south-eastern tip, west of Craighouse and between Lagg and Tarbert above the coast. The plantations largely consist of Sitka spruce and also include Lodgepole pine, Japanese larch, Scots and Corsican pines, Norway spruce and Douglas fir.

In terms of its vegetation, the exposed west coast of Jura is a different prospect to the more fertile low-lying areas to the island's east, and between autumn and spring the landscape here can appear almost barren. The most immediate contrast is the lack of tree cover. However, in spring there is a widespread eruption of vibrant green bracken ferns, swiftly followed by a profusion of bluebells. In season, clusters of sea pinks, primroses and varieties of orchid dot the shoreline, along with localised outbreaks of centaurium, grass of parnassus and other machair-type flowers – although there is little true machair to be found on Jura. 'Machair' is a Gaelic word referring to a low-lying fertile sand dune pasture found on some of the north-west coastlines of Ireland and Scotland – particularly the Outer Hebrides. Machair sand has a high seashell content and when blown inland it neutralises the acidity of peat soils, thereby propagating fertile grassland.

Much of Jura's interior consists of peat moor, which is prone to boggy conditions in some areas. Tussocky purple moor grass and mat grass are widespread as are bracken and heather on drier ground. Bog myrtle, bog asphodel, rushes and sedges such as cotton and deer grass thrive on the wetter ground. The island is also home to a number of bryophytes – mosses and liverworts – with Craighouse Ravine being especially propitious.

GETTING AROUND

The Jura bus service connects with the ferry from Port Askaig and runs from Feolin Ferry to Ardlussa. This is just over 35km (22 miles), but it takes around 1½hrs, partly on account of the rustic nature of the road. Details of corresponding bus times are given with the routes described below. The Jura Bus operates Monday to Saturday. For further information or to book connections with the mainland ferry, call Alex Dunnachie on 01496 820314 or 01496 820221. Private hire for individuals or groups of up to 16 is also catered for.

Mike Richardson operates a Landrover pick-up service from Ardlussa or Road End along the private track road to Kinuachdrachd. The cost is £40 from Ardlussa and £35 from Road End. Plenty of notice is advisable, tel 07899 912116.

It is possible to charter a boat into Glengarrisdale from Croabh Haven or Ruantallain from Port Askaig. Similarly, for those walking the west coast route who wish to avoid walking the 24km (15 miles) along the shores of Loch Tarbert, it should be possible to arrange a pick-up and drop-off by boat, between Ruantallain and Glenbatrick Bay. This is more viable for a small group. It is worth arranging boat charters well in advance of a trip. Farsain Cruises operates out of Croabh Haven – contact Duncan Philips on 01852 500644 or 07880 714165 – and for Islay Marine Charters, Port Askaig contact Roger Eaton on 01496 302459.

WHEN TO GO

In early spring and autumn you are more likely to benefit from mild weather, although rain can be a feature at any time of year. Another important advantage visiting in these seasons is that in early spring the bracken has not yet sprung up and in the autumn it dies back. Bracken forms a serious natural obstacle on parts of the west coast and is often festooned with deer ticks (see below). Furthermore, midges don't generally appear until late spring and disappear again in autumn.

In winter you're almost guaranteed to have the place to yourself, aside from Hogmanay, when Glengarrisdale often provides sanctuary for New Year refugees. If you're lucky you might enjoy some crystal-sharp, sun-lit winter days. It can be surprisingly mild in winter, thanks to the Gulf Stream. However, the weather can also be extremely rough. The terrain can be very boggy, with December and January being the wettest months on the island. Short winter days are another factor. It is doubly important to check the weather, let others know your planned route and be properly equipped before setting off for the west coast in winter. A round of the Paps should only be considered if the forecast is good.

In late spring and summer, you will have to contend with bracken and midges and you're less likely to have the place to yourself; as well as more walkers, many people arrive on the west coast by boat or kayak in

One of many burns to be crossed on the west coast of Jura

summer. In hot weather, walking over difficult terrain with a heavy pack can be gruelling. On the plus side, the days are long and evenings around a campfire are more viable. The ground

is generally less boggy and the colours can be fantastic – emerald green ferns cloak the island and when the bluebells are in bloom in late April or early May the combination is wonderful. The last weekend in May is a busy time, with the Isle of Jura fell race taking place. A recent innovation is the Ultra Marathon, which takes place around the same time and may involve parts of the west coast. If you appreciate the peaceful atmosphere of wild places, it's probably best to avoid this period.

ACCOMMODATION

The Jura Hotel is situated in the main village of Craighouse, overlooking Small Isles Bay. There are 18 rooms and the hotel has a dining room and lounge bar serving good fresh food based on local produce, including fresh fish and venison. There is a large garden to the front of the hotel where **camping** is permitted for a small donation. There are shower and laundry facilities at the hotel for non-residents, tel 01496 820243.

At Kinuachdrachd, Mike and Joan Richardson have a **walkers' bunkhouse** and also provide Bed and Breakfast in the farmhouse, tel 07899 912116. Other **B&B** and self-catering accommodation is listed in Appendix A.

There is an unofficial **camping area** at Corran Sands 5km (3 miles) north of Craighouse at the 'top' end of Small Isles Bay. A signpost indicates Corran Sands on the shore side of the road. There are no facilities. **Wild camping** is also permitted on Jura in accordance with the Land Reform (Scotland) Act 2003. However,

WILD CAMPING

According to The Scottish Outdoor Access Code: Access rights extend to wild camping. This type of camping is lightweight, done in small numbers and only for two or three nights in any one place. You can camp in this way wherever access rights apply but help avoid causing problems for local people and land managers by not camping in enclosed fields of crops or farm animals and keeping well away from buildings, roads or historic struc-

tures. Take extra care to avoid disturbing deer stalking or grouse shooting. If you wish to camp close to a house or building, seek the owner's permission. Leave no trace by: taking away all your litter; removing all traces of your tent pitch and of any open fire; not causing any pollution.

camping is restricted to areas where access rights are exercisable.

It is especially important to check with the estates before wild camping during the deer stalking season – between 1 July and 15 February.

There is also a **bothy** on the Ardlussa estate. The bothy is an old crofting cottage that was inhabited until after the Second World War though it is now maintained by the excellent Mountain Bothies Association (MBA), which looks after around 100 such refuges in remote and often mountainous environments in Scotland, as well as a few in northern England and Wales. The bothies are owned by landowners, who allow the MBA to maintain them as basic shelters for walkers, climbers and others. Maintenance work is carried out by work parties of volunteers. It is incumbent on those staying at a bothy to ensure that it is left in good order for the next users. There are two further estate bothies at Ruantallain and Cruib.

FOOD AND DRINK
As well as the Jura Hotel, the **Antlers Bistro and Restaurant** was opened in April 2009 and is situated opposite the shop and village hall in Craighouse. The Antlers also has a visitor centre. The **Jura Stores** is situated in the heart of Craighouse. Advanced orders are taken on 01496 820231 or shop@jurastores.co.uk If you need food and fuel for several days' walking on the west coast route you'll probably need to bring your own supplies. The **Isle**

of Jura distillery in Craighouse has a shop and runs twice-daily distillery tours from March to October and by appointment during the winter, tel 01496 820385, www.isleofjura.com.

WALKING THE WEST COAST OF JURA
The west coast of Jura route is not an established, well-defined, long-distance footpath starting at point A and finishing at point B. There are a number of alternative start and end points and the walk can vary from 48 to 89km (30 to 55 miles) in total. The route from Kinuachdrachd – near the northernmost point of the island – around the west coast to Ruantallain, then east to the road at the head of Loch Tarbert, is a well-rounded walk in its own right. However, there is much to recommend continuing west along the southern shore of the loch to Glenbatrick Bay and then carrying on either around the coast to Feolin Ferry or up through Glen Batrick past the Paps of Jura and on to the A846 7km (4 miles) north of Craighouse. Each of these routes is described in the guide.

Jura has few footpaths. The most notable, perhaps, is known as Evans' Walk and is named for Mr Henry Evans who established the Jura Forest deer hunting preserve in 1868. Evans had only one leg and the original path was constructed as a pony track so he could ride across his domain. The path is even marked on the OS Explorer map and recently had its own signpost erected at the A846 end. However, this does not make it a footpath in the sense familiar to residents of the Home Counties. While Evans' Walk is a distinct path for much of its length there are sections that are difficult to follow – particularly the last kilometre before the road where it often disappears into the boggy terrain.

Terrain

Chief among the difficulties facing west coast walkers is the often demanding terrain, combined with an almost total lack of paths and a complete absence of way-marking. Beyond Corryvreckan at the island's northern tip, the only tracks are those made by deer and wild goats, although these are often immensely useful. Generations of Jura's deer and feral goats have worked out the best

routes around the island's castellated and crenellated coastline and their tracks are generally worth following; they weave their ways efficiently through the broken, rocky terrain often encountered below the cliffs, contour around hillsides and find the easiest route around or across bogs or raised beaches. Indeed, in his book *Waterlog*, Roger Deakin suggests that 'hooves not boots' are the ideal equipment for walking here; on the same premise, four legs would also be useful and for that reason telescopic walking poles are recommended.

The terrain is boggy and tussocky at times and extensive bracken cover makes for particularly tough going during the summer. There are numerous burns to ford, beaches of fine sand or large pebbles to cross and steep-sided glens to negotiate. However, the

The start of Evans' Walk (Walk 3)

challenging nature of the terrain is also one of its great attractions; rather than tramping along a sedate, metalled and comprehensively signposted walker's motorway, there is much satisfaction in reading the landscape and plotting your own course through it.

However your route evolves, care should be taken, especially between Corryvreckan and Shian Bay, as there are numerous places where one can be drawn towards precipitous drops or along ultimately unnavigable stretches of shoreline. The Ordnance Survey 1:25,000 map (Explorer 355, Jura and Scarba) is essential equipment and a great help with route finding, but even with its topographical detail, it isn't always possible to assess whether a particular stretch of shoreline is passable.

Camping, bothying and bivvying

The nature of the terrain makes progress slower and more physically demanding than walking on established footpaths – particularly when carrying camping gear and several days' food – and this needs to be taken into account. For very fit individuals who have limited time, it is possible to eschew the camping option and walk from bothy to bothy – as will be described. Likewise, it is possible to bivouac in some of the numerous and often cavernous caves dotted along the shore, although many of these are carpeted with deer and goat droppings and often several decomposing examples of each species.

Combining camping and bothying is a good option. Hurrying between bothies limits opportunities to explore the environment and a tent increases one's options – such as the opportunity to camp at Shian Bay, which is possibly the most glorious wild-camping spot on the planet (see below). Furthermore, a tent is useful should you arrive to find a bothy fully occupied.

Drinking water can be collected from the burns which run off the hills at frequent intervals. The peaty soil gives the water an amber hue and a sweet flavour. I've never bothered purifying it and have never had a problem. However, make sure to collect your water from where the stream is visibly moving.

View from inside the bothy at Ruantallain (Walk 1, Day 3)

Driftwood is plentiful on most

beaches, though you may have to walk some distance to find adequate supplies. Try to leave a useful amount of firewood at the bothies for the next occupants. When camping, be careful not to let a fire get out of control and ensure that tents are pitched a safe distance upwind.

Obviously there is no refuse collection service from the bothies, so you are responsible for carrying your own rubbish out with you. Human waste should always be buried well away from bothies and water sources.

Beasties

The vast majority of Jura's wildlife is entirely benign, but there are a few exceptions. Deer ticks are ubiquitous from early spring through to late autumn and are often picked up when walking through bracken and long grass. Wearing shorts increases your chances of taking them onboard. These miniscule beasties burrow their heads into your flesh and are best removed with tweezers, but you must ensure that you remove the head when extracting them. Some ticks carry Lyme disease, which can become seriously debilitating if left undiagnosed. However, removal of infected ticks within 36 hours greatly reduces the risk of contracting Lyme disease.

Adders are common, though they are unlikely to bother you unless you bother them first. Be aware of them, however, as a bite can cause dizziness, vomiting, painful swelling and immobility of an affected limb – which can be a serious problem if you're a long and difficult walk away from treatment. Jellyfish are common in summer so be vigilant when enjoying a swim in one of the beautiful bays. Mice are often present at the various bothies, therefore it is important to hang food out of reach to avoid contamination and so as not to encourage them.

Midges are abundant on Jura between late spring and early autumn, and can seriously detract from one's enjoyment of the place, so be prepared if walking during this period. The Jura midge is the stormtrooper of the small-winged invertebrate world and in its tenacity and pathological aggression is matched only by the New Zealand sandfly.

Deerstalking season

If you set out to walk the west coast during the deer stalking season, which runs from 1 July until 15 February, then it is advisable to contact the estates where you will be walking, both for your own safety and as a matter of courtesy. The Barnhill Estate covers the northernmost part of the island, between An Carn on the east coast and Glengarrisdale on the west. Contact the Barnhill Estate on 01496 820327. The Ardlussa Estate covers the area south of the Barnhill Estate, with its southern boundary between Lussagiven on the east coast and Corpach Bay on the west. Contact the head keeper on 01496 820321. The Ruantallain Estate covers the area south of the Ardlussa Estate with its southern boundary along the north shore of Loch Tarbert. Contact the head keeper, Craig Rozga, on 01496 820287. The south shore of Loch Tarbert and the coastline south-west as far as Allt Bun an Eas (NR457763) is part of the Tarbert Estate, as is Glen Batrick and the Paps. Contact the head keeper, Gordon Muir, on 01496 820207. For the Inver Estate, which includes the stretch of coastline between Allt Bun an Eas and Feolin, call 01496 820223. For the Forest Estate, call 01496 820123.

THINGS TO TAKE BACKPACKING

The OS Explorer 1:25,000 sheet 355 is indispensable, as is a compass, walking poles, gaiters, sturdy boots, effective waterproofs, warm layers, a head torch, robust lightweight tent and good quality sleeping bag. An altimeter is also a useful navigational tool. It is tempting to think getting lost isn't possible when following the coastline, but it is often worth establishing exactly where you are, especially in poor conditions. Furthermore, being able to navigate is essential if for any reason you need to head east from the coast across the island's hilly interior to the road.

A Swiss army knife with tweezers comes in handy for tick-removal as well as for other uses. A few candles are always useful for evenings in a bothy. Lightweight binoculars are handy for admiring Jura's splendid wildlife. Serious insect repellents, mosquito coils and a midge/mosquito hat – or net to place over a hat – are useful lines of defence against *Culicoides impunctatis*, and some swear by Avon 'Skin So Soft' as a repellent. Mobile phone network coverage has increased on the west coast recently, but at the time of writing it is far from extensive. It is still worth taking a phone – as well as a basic medical kit and a survival bag – in case of misadventure.

WALK 1
The west coast walk
Main route – 5 Days, 77km (48 miles)

The track from Road End to Kinuachdrachd with Barnhill overlooking the Sound of Jura (Walk 1, Day 1)

There are three logical places to start the west coast walk, all on the east coast of the island. The first is Kinuachdrachd where the last vestiges of metalled track and the world of motorised transport are left behind. As described in 'Getting to the Southern Hebrides' in the Introduction, it is possible to arrive here by water taxi from the mainland. The alternative is to take the Jura Bus from Feolin or Craighouse to Ardlussa. From here it is 15km (9½ miles) along the track road to Kinuachdrachd and there are three options for getting there. The obvious choice is to walk. From Ardlussa, which comprises a handsome manor house and a collection of farm buildings and estate workers' houses (NR649879) – just follow the road north. The walk to Kinuachdrachd is pleasant, has a few minor ups and downs and should take around 3hrs. Barnhill is passed 2km before Kinuachdrachd.

Another option is to arrange transport as far as the small parking area at Road End – which is as far north as unauthorised vehicles are permitted. Kinuachdrachd is less than two hours walk from Road End. Alternatively, Mike Richardson can drive you from Ardlussa to Kinuachdrachd in his Landrover (see 'Getting around'

A NOTE OF CAUTION

I would strongly recommend that this walk should not be attempted by the very young or elderly or by anyone carrying an injury or who is otherwise unfit. Make sure someone knows of your planned route and your estimated time of completion. Check in by phone when you can. The high ground above Baigh Gleann Speireig, south-west of Glengarrisdale Bothy; the area around Shian Bay; the area just west of Ruantallain bothy and Glenbatrick Bay have mobile phone coverage.

section). Either way, if you arrive at Ardlussa on the afternoon bus (around 1700), then staying at the bunkhouse at Kinuachdrachd (see above) or camping at one of the nearby bays makes sense.

The walk is described here in a number of day stages. These stages are intended as a structure around which to build your own walk. Therefore, various options and alternatives are included along the way. How long you take to walk the west coast of Jura is contingent on a number of factors: how much time you have; your level of fitness; how much weight you are carrying; whether you are exclusively bothying; weather conditions; and the time of year. The height of the bracken, the conditions underfoot and the available daylight are additional seasonal factors. Fit walkers should manage Kinuachdrachd to Feolin Ferry in five to six days.

However, very fit and determined walkers might manage the route in three and a half days, for example:

- Day 1: Kinuachdrachd to Glengarrisdale
- Day 2: Glengarrisdale to Ruantallain
- Day 3: Ruantallain to Glenbatrick Bay
- Day 4 (half day): Glenbatrick to Feolin Ferry

In this guide, all timings given are estimates for fit walkers carrying 15–20kg and exclude breaks and detours. Allow more time where possible and remember that poor weather conditions, very wet ground and high bracken will all slow progress. It is also worth allowing yourself extra time for exploring this remarkable stretch of coastline; a week would be a good amount of time.

Day 1
Kinuachdrachd to Glengarrisdale

Distance	13km (8 miles)
Time	5–6hrs
Start	Kinuachdrachd harbour
	Grid ref: NR705982
Map	OS Explorer 355

This first leg of the west coast walk is not a great distance, but you will encounter some varied and challenging terrain. The going underfoot is often difficult and more so with a heavy pack. Once the 'path' runs out above the Gulf of Corryvreckan you will need to exercise caution and judgement in 'reading' the terrain to find good routes down to and along the west coast.

Whether arriving by boat or walking in from Ardlussa/ Road End, from Kinuachdrachd Harbour (NR705982) follow the track skirting the small bay north before ascending a little next to a tumbling burn and continuing on to **Kinuachdrachd**.

At Kinuachdrachd – which translates as 'headland above the ebb tide' – there is a lone farmhouse with a few outbuildings, including the bunkhouse. Just before arriving at the farmhouse on the track road, there is a footpath climbing to the left (NR704987). A small wooden sign announces the route to Corryvreckan, which is 3km to the north. The path, which can be boggy in places, climbs through heather and bracken before levelling out and passing through a deer fence by means of a stile and a kissing-gate. To the north, the isle of Scarba gradually detaches itself from the landmass of Jura as you approach **Corryvreckan**. It is worth watching out for sea eagles in this area. ▶

They are easily identifiable by their size (they boast a wing-span of up to 3m) and characteristic white tail feathers.

After 2km, the path passes through another deer fence then drops a little crossing a small gully and stream (NM701007). Here the path splits, but either route leads

45

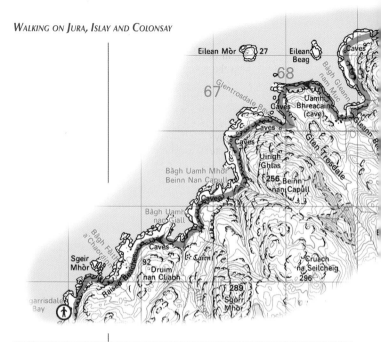

THE GULF OF CORRYVRECKAN

According to Norse legend, the Gulf of Corryvreckan (Breacan's Cauldron) takes its name from the son of a King of Norway who drowned here while attempting to win the love of a local woman by performing a feat of derring-do. Breacan anchored his boat in the strait for three days and nights using three ropes – the first of wool, the second of hemp and the third of a virgin's hair. The ropes broke in turn and the boat was dragged into the whirlpool. Breacan's dog dragged his lifeless body ashore and he was buried in a cave on the west coast.

In August 1947, when returning from a camping trip on the west coast with his three-year-old adopted son Richard, his sister Avril, two nephews and a niece, George Orwell steered his small boat into the gulf and rapidly got into difficulties. The boat's outboard motor was wrenched off in the violent tumult of water and disaster was narrowly forestalled when the party managed to scramble to safety on a small island after the boat capsized. Several hours later, they were rescued by a passing fishing boat.

to an obvious vantage point on the northern flank of An Cruachan, with superlative views of Scarba and the Gulf of Corryvreckan – the narrow strait between the two islands and the often turbulent confluence of the Firth of Lorn and the Sound of Jura. The tidal convergence of conflicting currents in the Gulf are catalysed by a submerged pyramidal rock, known as Caillich, The Hag, which generates an infamous whirlpool of considerable power.

From the vantage point on the northern flank of **An Cruachan**, contour west for 200m on a vague path that soon drops into the mouth of a wide gully running south to north off the hill. From here, make for a rock-walled gully below and a few hundred metres to the north-west. A burn runs down the gully, making it a little tricky to negotiate, but it provides a good point of access to the lower rock platform and the west coast.

Descending to the west coast from the flank of An Cruachan

Once you've arrived on the **west coast** you will find yourself in a landscape that is very different from the eastern
side of Jura. There are few trees and the vegetation is
largely comprised of bracken, heather, bog myrtle and
tussocky purple moor grass: species able to withstand
exposure and adapted to the acidic rock and soil. The
countenance of the west coast is altogether craggier than
the east; the exposed features of the formerly submarine
landscape are subjected to regular scouring by wind,
rain and sea. In winter weather this can seem a bleak
region indeed. On calm and bright days, however, the
essential ruggedness of the environment is intermittently
softened by white sandy beaches fringing turquoise bays.
In spring and summer, the verdant uncoiling bracken,
the brief but spectacular outburst of bluebells and the
scatterings of sea pinks and other seashore flowers also
lend the area a more benign air.

Between the northern end of the island and as far
south-west as Shian Bay, the terrain generally rises quite
steeply a short distance from the shore, except where
the glens open out onto bays and beaches. It is usually
possible to skirt around the promontories between bays
on the raised wave-cut platform, which intermittently
forms a rather wild undercliff walkway – though this often
involves negotiating a way through broken, rocky terrain and bracken. This is not as difficult as it sounds as
there are often established goat and deer tracks wending
through the terrain.

From the foot of An Cruachan, steer round to the
south on relatively level though often boggy ground
until you arrive at the first of the two coves forming **Bàgh
Gleann nam Muc** ('bay of the glen of the pigs'). Pick your
way around the fringe of the cove and descend to the first
of many beautiful sandy beaches that you will encounter.
Cross the beach and work your way through rocky terrain and bracken around the foot of the rocky outcrop
which bisects the bay, before arriving on a second sandy
beach. At the western end of this beach, you will arrive
at the neck of a promontory; here, you can cut across the

neck by way of a gentle – though often boggy – climb, due west through the obvious gap, before descending into **Glentrosdale Bay**. The alternative is to pick your way around the promontory above the shoreline. ▸

> Martin Martin, author of *A Description of the Western Islands of Scotland* (1703), visited Jura in 1695 and reported that the cave contained an altar and Breacan's tomb, but there are no traces of either remaining today. The cave has three stone walls protecting the entrance, which is some 13m wide.

This is worthwhile as there are a number of caves and rock arches along this stretch of the coastline including Uamh Bhreacain or Breacan's Cave, where the eponymous hero is purported to have been buried.

From Glentrosdale Bay, work your way around the next promontory through rocky, bracken-covered terrain for 1km and then, arriving at a spur blocking passage along the rock platform, follow an obvious deer path up a gully, along and down the other side to arrive at **Bàgh Uamh Mhór** ('bay of the big cave'). The bay is dominated by the craggy triumvirate of Beinn nan Capull, Cruach na Seilcheig and Sgorr Mhór (respectively: 'peak of the horses', 'hip-shaped hill of the snails' and 'big rock'), which are separated by twin steep-sided gullies running precipitously down to the shore.

Continue around the next, smaller promontory into **Bàgh Uamh nan Giall** ('bay of the cave of the hostages') where you will need to pick your way carefully over some large and often slippery boulders before crossing a beach of large cobbles. Once across, carry on round to a small and very beautiful sandy beach, which is perfect for a sheltered swim and makes for an idyllic bivouacking spot (NR664986).

If making for Glengarrisdale, however, cut across the neck of the low-lying Garbh Aird ('rough promontory') and continue on your way. The terrain is difficult to read at points during the next 2km, but the shoreline route is mostly navigable and animal tracks are again useful. Just beyond Garbh Aird, however, it is best to take to the higher ground along **Druim nan Cliabh** ('ridge of the chests') to avoid a tricky stretch of slippery rocks, awkward slopes and boggy ground. After a few hundred

Quartz vein in the quartzite rock

metres, find your way down off the ridge alongside the burn (NR658977) feeding into the aptly named Feith a' Chaorainn ('bog of the rowan'). Once you're clear of the boggy terrain, stay as close to the shore as you can because there are some fine geological features on the way to Glengarrisdale including several splendid quartz-veined rock faces.

After a further 1km, you should catch sight of the white walls and red roof of Glengarrisdale bothy, on the far side of the bay, although it takes longer than you might antici-pate to actually reach **Glengarrisdale Bay**. On arrival, cross the beach to the outflow of the Glengarrisdale River, which fans out where it meets the beach, and ford it here, at its shallowest point. Alternatively you can batter your way through the bracken and follow the river-bank around to two trees standing 100m south-east of the bothy; here there are some stepping stones across a ford (NR644968), though it is difficult to cross here when the river is in spate.

GLENGARRISDALE BOTHY

The bothy is an old crofting cottage that was inhabited until after the Second World War. The bothy is on the Ardlussa estate, though it is now maintained by the excellent Mountain Bothies Association (MBA). Glengarrisdale bothy has two rooms and a tool store downstairs with the attic space given over for sleeping. Some sleeping platforms have recently been installed in the down-stairs rooms. One of the downstairs rooms has a hearth, the other a small pot-bellied stove. There tends not to be much driftwood in Glengarrisdale Bay, so you may have to retrace your steps a bit to gather some. If you arrive well before nightfall, or if you're staying for a while, then a driftwood gather-ing expedition to Baigh Gleann Speireig (which is around 20mins from the bothy by the direct route – see below), may be in order. The water from Glengarrisdale River is safe to drink.

Walkers at Glengarrisdale bothy

Glengarrisdale Bay is a wonderful spot, whatever the time of year or weather conditions; when it is fair there are fine views out over the bay towards Iona, Mull, the Garvellachs and Scarba and on a clear night the canopy of stars is beguiling. In wind and rain the rocky coastline is magnificent, especially when admired from within the bothy with a driftwood fire ablaze in the hearth. If you hang around Glengarrisdale with your binoculars you've a good chance of seeing some interesting birds, such as merlins, short-eared owls and hen harriers. Common and Atlantic grey seals frequently bob around in the bay and otters patrol close to the shore. Deer come down to the shore in the evening to graze on the kelp and some say that the seaweed in their diet gives Jura venison a distinctive flavour. During the rutting season of late September and October your dreams may be infiltrated by the throaty barking of hormonal stags.

Although there are no traces remaining today, Glengarrisdale was once home to **Aros Castle**, a stronghold of the Macleans for several centuries. The Macleans once held the entire northern half of Jura, but in 1745 the land was forfeit because of their loyalty to the Stuart cause. In 1647 Glengarrisdale was the scene of a battle between the Macleans and the Campbells and many of the Macleans were killed. A human skull believed to be a relic of the battle sat for many years under a shelf of rock in a cave known as Maclean's Skull. Local belief held that if the skull was moved it would always return to the same spot. It disappeared in 1976.

DAY 1 ALTERNATIVE
Road End to Glengarrisdale

Distance	7km (4½ miles)
Time	2hrs
Start	Disused quarry at Road End
	Grid ref: NR671928
Map	OS Explorer 355

Although the distance is not great, this can be a tough walk especially in boggy conditions with a heavy pack.

From the parking area in a disused quarry at Road End continue on the track road north-east on an incline for 1km. The track levels then drops a little and after a further few hundred metres you will arrive at a chain strung across the road (NR676943). At this point turn off the track to your left and head north-west across open country; you should be able to follow prominent all-terrain vehicle (ATV) tracks across the boggy ground, descending slightly and crossing a couple of burns. ▸

After crossing another larger burn, follow the ATV tracks north-west as the

Caution is required as the ground can be very boggy. The ATV tracks may become indistinct at times, so keep map and compass to hand.

ground rises a little. After a short distance the track levels and brings you into an open area; continue for 100m then look out for a track bending to your left around a knoll and then climbing the shoulder of a low hill to the west. Once you're on this track it will take you above the northern end of **Loch a' Gheiodh** ('loch of the

53

*Heading west
from Road End to
Glengarrisdale*

goose') and then drop to the northern tip of **Loch Doire na h-Achlaise** ('loch of the grove of the armpit-shaped bend', NR656961). The track climbs again then contours around the flank of Clachaig Mheadhoin, crosses a low col then turns to the left descending steeply through bracken. Following the track can be difficult when the bracken is up and if you do lose it the trick is not to stay up on the hillside too long, but to find a manageable route down into the glen.

The gradient eases and the path bends right, levels out and heads north into **Glen Garrisdale**. After a short while the track becomes less distinct as it crosses a boggy area before turning left and descending to a metalled path, which makes for a gap in a dry-stone wall crossing Glengarrisdale from east to west. From here head just east of north making for the gap in a second dry-stone wall a few hundred metres further on across open ground. Just beyond this wall two trees stand next to a ford with stepping stones across the Glengarrisdale River (NR644968), 100m south-east of the white-walled and red-roofed bothy. ◄

If the river is in spate, you may be better off following the riverbank around to its outflow on the beach, 300m to the north-east.

ONLY ONE SAILOR

If you find this stage hard going, reflect on the endeavour of Kate Johnson who lived on the croft at Glengarrisdale during the Second World War. Discovering the body of a German seaman washed ashore, she carried the corpse across the island and delivered it to the authorities. As Peter Youngson records: 'She was paid a small bounty for her trouble, and was later asked by a local inhabitant how she had managed such a feat of strength, and how she felt about it all. She was reported as having been unperturbed by the experience, but expressed some disappointment that there had only been the one sailor!' (Peter Youngson, Jura: *Island of Deer*, Birlinn, 2001)

Day 2
Glengarrisdale to Shian Bay

Distance	19km (12 miles)
Time	7–9hrs
Start	Glangarrisdale Bothy
	Grid ref: NR644969
Map	OS Explorer 355

This is a big day's walk; the distance is not especially great, but the terrain is very demanding. A fit walker could manage the 24km (15 miles) to the bothy at Ruantallain in a day (8–10hrs, assuming you take the 'clifftop' route to Ruantallain from Shian Bay), although taking the time to enjoy this beautiful stretch of coastline is recommended. There are fine opportunities for a bivouac en route although Shian Bay is the best of all.

There are two options on leaving Glengarrisdale. Firstly, steering a course around the coast to Baigh Gleann Speireig ('bay of the glen of the sparrowhawk') is a stimulating walk. At the north-western end of Glengarrisdale Bay, follow the goat tracks that weave through the initially

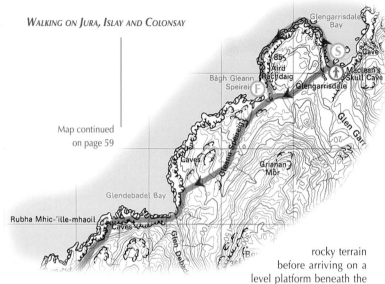

Map continued
on page 59

rocky terrain before arriving on a level platform beneath the cliffs. Continue on this easy terrain as the coastline bends southwards. There is a fine rock arch a few hundred metres north of Baigh Gleann Speireig, which is 2km around the coast from Glengarrisdale.

The second option is to cut across the neck of the promontory between Glengarrisdale and Baigh Gleann Speireig. Head west from the north end of the bothy, climbing a little and keeping to the area between the higher ground to north and south. Where the terrain levels out, there are a number of old peat cuttings and the ground can be boggy. Continue west dropping down to the bay. This latter route is less interesting, but will save you half an hour or so. Probably the first thing you'll notice at Baigh Gleann Speireig, is the accumulated flotsam and jetsam. There's usually plenty of driftwood to be had here, but sadly an alarming amount of plastic rubbish also comes ashore.

From Baigh Gleann Speireig there are two options. Firstly you can work your way around the coast for a few hundred metres and then – exercising care – find a way up onto the cliffs, as the rocky point at the western extremity of Port na Spuir is impassable. Alternatively, you can

make your way directly up onto higher ground through Gleann Speireig. Keep right of the Allt Gleann Speireig as you climb and keep Cnoc Carrach an Aoinidh Fhiadhta to your left. Once over the top, as the ground begins to drop towards the steep-sided glen that opens out into Glendebadel Bay (from the Norse, meaning 'deep dale'), make for the point where Glendebadel Burn reaches the beach (NR623951) and you will find an easy way down. Once the burn has been crossed, it is worth continuing along the undercliff platform for a while. ▶ After 500m you will encounter a spur with animal tracks running invitingly up a gully – ignore this and skirt around the spur. A few hundred metres further on you will come to another spur. This time follow the tracks up the gully (NR614950).

On the other side of the spur lies another inviting undercliff world, but there is an impassable cliff a few hundred metres further along, so continue up to higher ground above the cliffs. Find a comfortable line and contour along at around 100m for the next 1km, crossing a burn before gaining Cnoc na h-Uamha (110m, NR608941). Descend and cross another burn, climbing again to around 100m and contouring for another 1km before climbing to the landward shoulder of Stac Dearg

Traigh à Mhiadair and Corpach Bay

There is much to admire and weaving a route through the broken, rocky terrain by means of deer and goat tracks is highly entertaining.

(130m, NR594935). Skirt a small lochan, then contour along, tending south for a few hundred metres. Below to the west the Garbh uisge nan Cad burn flows through a gully. There is an obvious point at which to descend and cross the burn, before it drops precipitously into a steep-sided gorge (NR591931).

After crossing the burn, climb west-south-west until you reach level ground with another burn trickling along rather sedately. Cross the burn and continue west for a few hundred metres until you arrive at a natural amphitheatre, facing out to sea between Rubh' a Bhaile-dhoire ('point of the shut-in town') and Rubha Lag Losguinn ('point of the hollow of the frogs', NR582927). Follow the goat tracks leading down the springy peat-turfed slopes to the beach.

The next few kilometres

include some of Jura's most beautiful coastline. From Rubha Lag Losguinn, take advantage of the goat

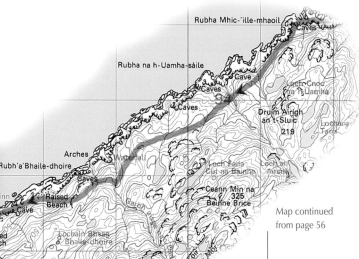

Map continued
from page 56

tracks
to pick a
route through
the rocky and
bracken-infested terrain
and, after clonking across
a large-pebbled beach, you will
eventually emerge onto the magnificent
Corpach Bay. ▶

If the weather is
rough and you don't
have the energy or
inclination to step on
as far as Ruantallain
bothy, then Corpach
Bay may be a better
bivouac site than
Shian Bay.

The name **Corpach** is from the Gaelic meaning
'body' or 'corpse' and long ago corpses of notables
were carried here across the island to await transporta-
tion to Iona or Oronsay, which were important ecclesiastical centres. Coffins were often kept in the caves
awaiting suitable conditions for the voyage. Corpach
Bay possesses a beautiful sandy beach and makes for
a wonderful bivouacking site. There is plenty of shelter,
a burn, flat grassy areas for pitching a tent and usually
plenty of driftwood to be gleaned.

The sweep of Corpach Bay continues for around
1km and arriving at its south-western end you will find
the rock stacks, arches, caves and steeply-sloped sand

JULIE BROOK

The environmental artist Julie Brook lived in a rock arch near Corpach Bay for several periods during the early 1990s, including an entire year between April 1993 and April 1994. Julie had supplies delivered by fishing boat and aside from occasional forays into the teeming metropolis of Craighouse, she lived a solitary existence with only her cat for company. Julie produced a number of large impressionistic paintings which she later exhibited in Craighouse, as well as ephemeral sculptural pieces including 'firestacks' – driftwood fires set on top of stacks built from large pebbles at low tide, which would appear to become floating islands of fire as the tide came in.

dunes of Tràigh a' Mhiadair. Beyond the south-western end of Tràigh a' Mhiadair it is best to take to the clifftops for the next few kilometres until you come to the fine, stepped waterfall at Sliabh Allt an Tairbh (NR544893). It is possible to descend to the shore again here and the undercliff route makes for easier and more interesting walking to Shian Bay. It can be tricky crossing the outflow of the waterfall, which runs out through a narrow gorge for some distance. When the tide is high it may be

Waterfall at Sliabh allt an Tairbh

difficult to pass in front of a low cliff encountered shortly after crossing the burn. Alternatively, you can continue along the clifftops to Shian Bay from here, but the going can be fairly tough.

Presently, you will arrive at Shian Bay 2.5km beyond Sliabh Allt an Tairbh. The bay is a beautiful white sand crescent backed by a flat grassy area and protected to the north by Shian Island. The Shian River flows out into the middle of the bay and to the rear the land opens out, rising more gradually from the shore to the hills in the interior. Shian is the Gaelic for 'fairy' and on a clear evening the place has such a magical quality that the appearance of sprites along the shore would seem entirely in keeping. This is a wonderful spot for a bivouac and there's usually abundant driftwood to be had. A tent will be very vulnerable here in strong winds, although there are caves around for emergency shelter. If the water isn't too cold or you are blessed with a Caledonian insensitivity to challenging temperatures, Shian Bay is an idyllic place for a swim.

DAY 3
Shian Bay to Cruib Lodge

Distance	13km (8 miles)
Time	5hrs
Start	Shian Bay
	Grid ref: NR531875
Map	OS Explorer 355

If you opt to walk from Shian Bay to Cruib Lodge, take at least a few hours to explore the environs of Ruantallain. This is a region of such outstanding natural beauty that it is worth factoring an extra day into your itinerary and spending the night here. A good option is to walk from Shian bay ▸

to Runtallain bothy above the shore – which should take 1½hrs – and then head back beneath the cliffs to explore, having deposited your rucksack at the bothy. There are two options for the route between Ruantallain and Cruib Lodge. The 'inland' route is slighlty quicker and follows ATV tracks for much of its length, though it can be boggy at times. The coastal route takes longer and is harder going, but is full of interesting geological phenomena and wildlife spotting opportunities.

Shian Bay to Ruantallain

Head south-west across the beach, crossing the outflow of the Shian River if you haven't already done so. Look out for the obvious ATV tracks exiting the beach to the east and follow these away from the shore for 100m or so, before turning south-west off the tracks again and setting off across country.

Above Shian Bay the land opens out before climbing to the mountainous hinterland.

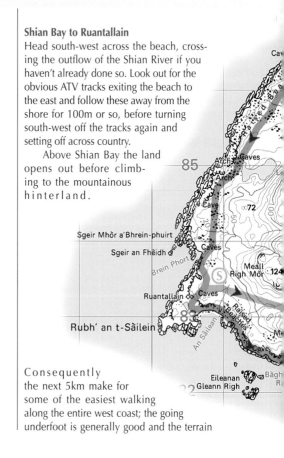

Consequently the next 5km make for some of the easiest walking along the entire west coast; the going underfoot is generally good and the terrain is relatively level, with only one real incline to be tackled. However, you should attempt to steer a course that avoids crossing large sections of the magnificent raised beaches that are abundant in this area (see the 'Geology' section above). Crossing these broad swathes of large pebbles is very hard work, especially with a large pack. You should be able to pick out animal tracks that work their way between the raised beaches, cleave to their edges and cross their narrowest points – as deer also find the cobbles tricky underhoof.

Looking west when traversing this section of the coast gives views over to **Colonsay** and, at its southern extremity, the distinct bump of **Oronsay**. To the south-west there are views out along the craggy point of Rubh'

63

an t-Sáilein ('point of the salt' – 'Ruantallain' being its anglicisation) and on to the coast of **Islay** with Rhuvaal Lighthouse standing vigil at that island's north-eastern extremity. To the south, once the slightly elevated ground has been cleared, grand views of the **Paps** are to be had. Rising to the east are **Dubh Bheinn**, **Rainberg Mor** and **Cruib**, with their curious, oblique striations carved out of the rock by the grinding passage of the ice-cap. Closer to hand, the route through the raised beaches passes a number of **lochans** of varying sizes to the landward side. In a certain light, their peat-dark waters appear almost black.

A couple of kilometres beyond Shian Bay, there is an old Landrover track that is worth following as it makes for easier going underfoot and plots an efficient course south-west towards Ruantallain. The track turns sharply south-east just north of **Breinn Phort** for a couple of hundred metres before turning south-west again and passing along the clifftop above the bay. Continue along the track as it crosses an area of raised beach and then curves around to the south-east. Looking south from a bend in the track (NR505837), there is a small, pointed hillock with a large dry-stone-walled enclosure a short distance to the right. There is a faint path leading between these two features, which then drops through a rocky outcrop, before arriving at the rear of the **Ruantallain bothy**.

The **bothy** itself is at the eastern end of a long corrugated iron-roofed house belonging to the Ruantallain Estate. The main part of the house is private and is locked when not in use. The bothy's single room has three small, ancient iron bed frames, a table, a fireplace and a small south-facing window. There are usually some crates and boards around to make some seats. The walls and ceiling are wood-panelled and the place comes into its own with a fire in the grate. There are several beaches for gathering driftwood – the eastern end of An Sàilean bay, south-east of the bothy, is the best.

A dry-stone wall in front of the bothy encloses a level grassy area, which is ideal for pitching tents. Some 50m south of the enclosure is a lochan, which serves as the fresh-water supply for the bothy.

Ruantallain bothy

Exploring Ruantallain
A couple of hundred metres south-east of Ruantallain, the ground climbs to the grassy hillock of Ceannaiche Mor, a fine vantage point with a 360° view. With patience and the right conditions, the rocky terrain beneath Ceannaiche Mor to the west and south-west is good for fishing, seal and otter spotting, and watching the sun set behind Colonsay.

Heading north-east around the coast from Ruantallain delivers you into a realm of fascinating geological phenomena; within a few metres of the bothy there are raised sea-caves and rock stacks to explore. Between Ruantallain and Shian Bay, the seaward edge of what geologists call the High Rock Platform forms the 10–15m high cliffline of the Main Rock Platform. This platform is also continuous north from Shian Bay to Glendebadel Bay where it is associated with cliffs that are up to 100m high.

The shoreline from Ruantallain is passable almost all the way to Shian Bay, although a few hundred metres north of the bothy it is advisable to follow the gully at Glac nam Bòcan (NR506835) up onto the clifftop before descending again at **Brein Phort** bay. It is possible to negotiate this section beneath the cliffs at low tide, but only for the lithe and sure-footed, as a little rock climbing is involved.

Brein Phort bay is a paradise for beachcombers as it attracts more flotsam and jetsam than any other beach on Jura. However, among the rusting marker buoys, driftwood and fish crates there is a large volume of plastic rubbish, most notably water bottles. Brein Phort means 'rotten port', either because of its exposure or because of the smell of decay. The name is comprehensible in both senses as the bay offers little shelter in rough weather and quantities of seaweed and expired deer, goats, seals and occasional dolphins are to be found decomposing there.

Tribes of wild goats are frequently encountered along this stretch and will generally flee as soon as they get wind of you.

Further north-east around the coast from Brein Phort, there are numerous rock stacks, natural arches and caves – and some of the latter are literally cavernous. There is so much to admire and explore along this stretch of coast that it can easily take three hours to walk to Shian Bay from Ruantallain. ◄ Like the deer that roam along the

Coastline near Ruantallain

west coast, these shaggy-coated, magnificently-horned beasts have the knack of arraying themselves portentiously against the clifftop skyline for maximum effect. Anyone who has ever eaten goat's cheese will recognise the attendant aroma of Jura's wild goats.

Ruantallain to Cruib Lodge by the 'inland' route

Continuing on from Ruantallain, the west coast route heads east, either above or along the north shore of Loch Tarbert. The former option (marked in blue on the map) is arguably the easier and quicker of the two, taking between two and three hours depending on conditions. From Ruantallain bothy, head north-east, up through the rocky terrain to the rear of the bothy and pick up the obvious ATV track heading east. Follow this track up hill and down dale and it will eventually deliver you to the environs of Cruib Lodge. This track is mostly well defined, though a bit indistinct in places and intersected by a number of other tracks along the way. It can also be very boggy in places.

The track is marked on the OS Explorer map and, dropping into and climbing out of Gleann Righ Mór and Gleann Righ Beag (the glens of the big and wee kings respectively) en route, it follows a trend just south of east until it turns north-east just before dropping down again to cross the **Garbh Uisge** ('rough water') burn. The track continues on a north-easterly trend, gaining height again after crossing Garbh Uisge, then wiggling around a bit until it arrives at a point (NR563832) north-west of the **Cruib Lodge** bothy, which will not as yet be visible. However, there is a plantation of young trees to its rear, protected by deer fences; once you have this in your sights you can strike out south-east across country, aiming for the bottom end of the enclosure and then following the burn around to the bothy itself. Keep your compass and map handy during this leg of the walk and you shouldn't encounter any problems. In clear weather, this route provides splendid views of Loch Tarbert, the Paps and Glen Batrick to the south; Ruantallain, north-eastern Islay and Colonsay to the West and Cruib to the north-east. The track also passes by a number of fine lochans.

Ruantallain to Cruib Lodge around the coast

Cruib Lodge can also be reached by forging a route along the shore. At 3–3½hrs it is a slightly longer and perhaps more difficult option than the route described above, but it has compensations. It largely avoids the bogginess endemic to the higher ground during wet periods. There is also much more shelter available in wet and windy weather. Furthermore, as far as Rubha Gille nan Ordag, it is also a very beautiful and interesting stretch of coastline.

Once at the bay, it's worth following the deer tracks which skirt or cross the pebble beaches and pick routes through the bracken.

For the shoreline route, when leaving Ruantallain bothy, head south-east to An Sàilean bay avoiding the boggy ground immediately to the east of the lochan. ◄ An enormous and spectacular raised beach sits above Rubha Buidhe, the rocky point which flanks An Sàilean bay to the east. A few hundred metres beyond Rubha Buidhe you will gain the rocky undercliff platform beneath Creag nan Seabhag.

The next 1km or so involves some enjoyable clambering about through broken, rocky terrain and slipping through notches in the numerous natural dikes. The cliffs along this stretch are dotted with caves, including Uamh Righ, the King's Cave (NR515827), which is found just before the coastline bends north-east into Bàgh Gleann Righ Mór.

Basalt dike at Ruantallain

On excavating **King's Cave** in 1971, the palaeontologist John Mercer recorded that '[b]attered onto the walls are well over a hundred poorly made crosses'. Today there are no actual crosses, although there are a number of rough cruciform etchings on the cave walls, lending Uamh Righ an eerie atmosphere. Mercer's archaeological finds, including simple tools and animal bones, link the west coast's caves with human habitation back to the Early Iron Age. He also suggests that some islanders may have sought refuge in the caves after the Clearances.

Continue along the undercliff platform into **Bàgh Gleann Righ Mór** and on to the pebble beach, which is best traversed by means of deer tracks. Follow the tracks along the bay and continue around the **Aird Reamhar** promontory, which has some impressive dikes, into the next bay. A rock-clad hillock above the promontory drops its shoulder down to the shore on the west side of the bay, obliging walkers to pick their way around its rocky flank, above the shore. The rocks are slippery when wet and pitched steeply enough to be hazardous.

Carry on around the bay and along the shoreline as it strikes out to the south-east, seemingly making for the southern shore of Loch Tarbert. At **Rubha Liath** ('grey point'), with its series of obliquely-angled dikes, there are good views south-east across the loch to the impressive raised beach forming a natural dam between Lochan Maol an t-Sornaich ('wee loch of the round hill of the chimney') and Loch Tarbert.

Beyond Rubha Liath, work your way around the bay of Port Falaith a' Chumhainn Mór, keeping a lookout for some navigation pillars (metre-high obelisks, white-painted on their seaward faces) above Rubha Gille nan Ordag at the eastern end of the bay (NR543814). This is a good point at which to leave the shore behind and make for higher ground. East of Rubha Gille nan Ordag the shoreline becomes estuarine, relatively uninteresting and very difficult to walk around. Therefore, climb above the shore and plot a course north-east along a line of hillocks

Heading east above the north shore of Loch Tarbert with Cruib (315m) dominating the horizon

that run parallel to the north shore as it angles sharply away from the south shore of Loch Tarbert.

Once you're up, try to avoid dropping down too far between the hillocks, thus avoiding boggy ground where possible. After 1km or so this route will lead you down into the glen through which the **Garbh Uisge** burn flows. Once you've crossed the burn, pick up the ATV tracks and follow the route described in the Ruantallain to Cruib Lodge 'inland' route itinerary above.

> **Cruib Lodge** is on the Ruantallain Estate and is used at times as a bothy by estate staff. Like the bothies at Glengarrisdale and Ruantallain, it is available for public use. The bothy itself is one of the building's three rooms, the other two being used for storage. There is a fireplace, table and two bed frames slung with netting. Above the deer-fenced tree plantation, the burn can be followed upstream, alongside the gorge it descends, to a beautiful small waterfall and plunge pool, which makes for a wonderful al fresco shower – though only out of midge season!

DAY 4
Cruib Lodge to Glenbatrick Bay

Distance	16km (10 miles) to Glenbatrick Bay; 6.5km (4 miles) to Loch Tarbert
Time	6–8hrs to Glenbatrick Bay; 2–3hrs to the A846 at the head of Loch Tarbert
Start	Cruib Lodge bothy Grid ref: NR567829
Map	OS Explorer 355

This is arguably the toughest section of the west coast walk as the going underfoot is often boggy and tussocky. The terrain can be difficult to read in places, and as the route is largely away from the shore route finding is often less obvious than when walking along the coast proper. Keep map and compass handy. Though rough, this section recompenses endeavour with some impressive landscapes.

To the rear of Cruib Lodge there is a small plantation of trees protected by deer fences; skirt around to the east of this enclosure and look for an ATV track bearing north-east. Follow this track for around 500m, before turning east and descending through an obvious gap (NR570834) to the mud and sand flats of Learadail. From here it is best to head for the southern end of Loch na Pearaich, which is 1500m to the east, though not visible until you are almost upon it. From the western side of Learadail, cross the outflow of the burn where it is shallowest and head south-east to pass through the gap at the neck of the promontory flanking Learadail to the east. Cross the mud flats of Sàilean nam Màireach, making for the small waterfall which is the outflow of Loch na Pearaich. Climb just north of east for a few hundred metres and you will arrive at the loch; it is then best to skirt around to its northern end before continuing.

On reaching the northern tip of Loch na Pearaich you will find an ATV track to follow south-east, down a slope onto a small boggy plateau – if you get across this with dry feet you will be doing well. Having crossed this area, look for a vague path heading north-east without losing any height. After 300m you should be contouring along the hillside with the mud and sand flats at the head of Loch Tarbert some 40m below to your right. Look out for a small salient of dry land bulging out into the estuary's mud flats (NR594836); there is a rough path that descends diagonally north-east to this point.

Arriving at the bottom of the slope, skirt around the edge of the mud flats to the north-east for around 800m, making for a weir and a rickety footbridge (NR598843). Cross the bridge and follow the obvious path – marked with white-painted stones – to the point where it divides after

100m. If you are finishing your walk here, then follow the white-painted stones along the left-hand branch, which climbs a low hill and makes for the A846, 1500m further on. If continuing on, the right-hand branch soon becomes vaguer, though it's easy enough to follow as it steers a course more or less around the head of the loch. After another 1km you can cut across the neck of a small inlet called Cairidh Bheag (NR598829) when the tide is out or use the stepping stones further up

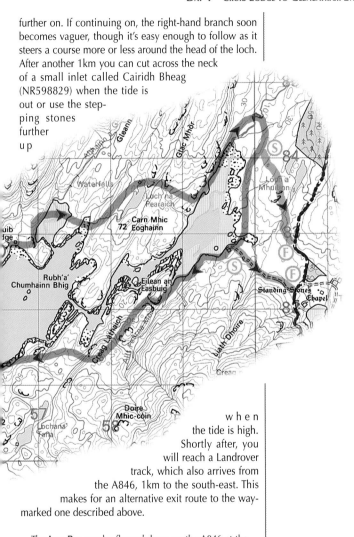

w h e n the tide is high. Shortly after, you will reach a Landrover track, which also arrives from the A846, 1km to the south-east. This makes for an alternative exit route to the way-marked one described above.

The **Jura Bus** can be flagged down on the A846 at the point where the track from the settlement at Tarbert joins the road. This is 300m south-east of where the way-marked route meets the road and 100m north-east of where the Landrover track joins it. From Monday through to Saturday the bus passes Tarbert at around 0900 and 1700 though it is best to be there in advance and times should be checked with the Jura Bus Company – contact details above.

For those continuing on to Glenbatrick Bay, follow the Landrover track down to the shore and past a boat house until it peters out after a few hundred metres, or at high tide use the path next to the boat house that stays above the high-water line. Continue west along the shoreline into Bàgh an Uillt Fhearna. There are stepping stones crossing the burn that runs into the bay from the south – cross here and climb directly south-west onto the low ridge that boundaries the west side of the bay. It is best to take to the higher ground here as the lower ground is boggy and tussocky and the shoreline is not particularly interesting.

Once you're atop the ridge, cross over to its west side and follow the deer tracks that run south-west along the ridge. Continue for about 1km, contouring or gaining and losing a little height, until you are a few hundred metres south-west of a U-shaped bay some way along the steep flank of **Creag Làthaich** ('rock of the swamp', NR576814); descend here with care and head north-west across the boggy open ground towards the obvious gap between areas of raised ground. Climb a little then contour just south of west along a small ridge, crossing a burn and skirting the flank of a small hill before descending to the shore just north-east of Sgeir na Muic-mara (NR568814). Continue south-west following the shore on level ground for around 1500m before arriving at the dammed lochan and beach at **Cairidh Mhor**. The dam can be walked across with care in dry weather; alternatively, walk around the lochan to be on the safe side.

Once over, continue around to the westernmost side of the bay and then, following deer tracks, climb to the west gaining 30m and passing just north of a small

lochan (NR552807) beneath **Cnoc Rubh' a' Choire**. Keep heading west until you're looking down on **Lochan Maol an t-Sornaich** and its massive pebble beach. Tending north of west, follow some obvious deer tracks down to the north-east end of the beach. This beach is an absolute marvel in terms of its scale and nature. Its setting between Lochan Maol an t-Sornaich and Loch Tarbert is quite magnificent.

Maol an t-Sornaich

▶ As you progress south-west along the top of the beach the pebbles become ever larger. At the south-western extremity of the beach, climb up onto the rocky knolls before dropping down to cross the **Abhainn Luindale** ('river of the spring') at a point above the waterfall (NR543804). You should be able to cross over using rocks as stepping stones, but exercise caution. Alternatively, the river can be crossed near the shore, but this can be a boots-off affair.

On arriving at the beach you will notice how smooth, beautiful and curiously patterned the small pebbles are.

Having crossed the river, head for the shore and then continue on your way around the coast, skirting pebble beaches, picking your way through broken rocky terrain and crossing several natural dikes. After 1500m you should arrive at a small sandy bay just beyond **Rubh' a' Bhàillein** ('point of the walls'); the shoreline is rocky to the south-west, but you should be able to pass in front of these rocks at low tide. When the tide is high, find a route landward of the rocks. Either way, continue for a few hundred metres until you arrive at the **Glenbatrick**

River. The river is best crossed by means of a footbridge a few hundred metres upstream from its outflow. Once you've crossed the bridge, follow the path to the **house**, which sits sentinel-like in the middle of Glenbatrick Bay, keeping watch over Loch Tarbert and Ruantallain. To the rear of the house, Glen Batrick climbs between the slopes of Beinn Bhreac ('speckled peak') and Scrinadle (from the Norse for 'scree') with the great, dark dome of Beinn Shiantaidh dominating its upper reaches.

> The **house** is Victorian and was built as a hunting lodge; today it is a summer residence of the Astor family, owners of the Tarbert Estate. It is occupied mainly during the summer months, but it may also be in use at other times. The house is also connected with an infamous disappearing act. Local legend has it that when the Profumo Scandal hit the headlines in 1963, Christine Keeler and her friend Mandy Rice-Davies were spirited away from London and hidden away at Glenbatrick. John Profumo, Secretary of State for War in the Conservative government, was a good friend of Lord Astor, himself a Tory cabinet minister at that time.

When the house is not occupied there are good camping spots outside the garden walls. If it is in use, however, then choose your camping spot at a discreet distance. The river is your water supply and there's usually some driftwood to be had along the shore. Glenbatrick is pronounced locally as Glen-a-batrick, reflecting its original name of Glenabedrig, which derives from the Norse *beit-ar* meaning 'pasture' and *vik* meaning 'harbour'.

The Tarbert Estate hunting lodge at Glenbatrick Bay

Day 5

Glenbatrick Bay to Feolin Ferry around the coast

Distance	16km (10 miles)
Time	5–6 hours
Start	Glenbatrick
	Grid ref: NR518800
Map	OS Explorer 355

The walk from Glenbatrick Bay to Feolin Ferry is generally easier going than the previous section, but it is far from the proverbial stroll in the park. You will encounter a variety of terrain and there many interesting geological phenomena along the route.

Rejoin the path running east to west behind the house and continue west as it becomes a more definite ATV track. The track bends north of west and climbs a slope at the western end of the bay; stay with the track as the coast beyond **Rubhachan Eoghainn** (Hugh's Points) is unnavigable for some distance and where it is navigable it can be very hard going on large cobbles.

Atop the slope, the path continues west for 500m, skirting a magnificent raised beach. It then bends south and forks; take the right-hand fork and cross the **Allt Beithe** burn. After a further 100m or so, the track bends south-west and begins to climb more steeply. At this point (NR504801), choose a route off the main track – there may be deer tracks – north-west across Maol a' Chrois Aoinidh ('the brow of the cross cliff') until you're above the clifftops. It is possible to descend to the shore at **Rubh' a' Chrois-aoinidh** (NR503805), depending on the tide, and the undercliff platform is magnificent along this stretch, but in rough weather or at high tide this route can become impassable and dangerous near Rubh' a' Chrois-aoinidh. This being the case, contour your way around to

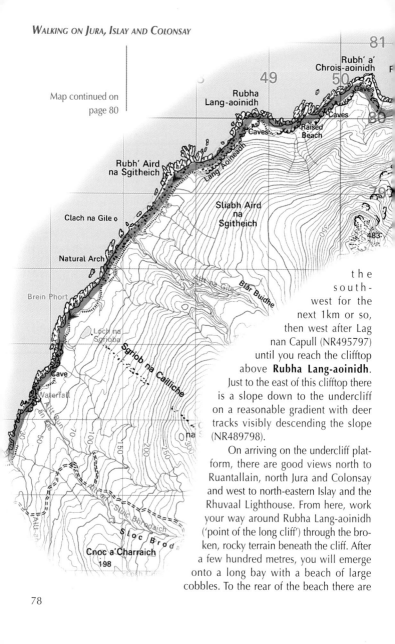

Map continued on
page 80

the south-west for the next 1km or so, then west after Lag nan Capull (NR495797) until you reach the clifftop above **Rubha Lang-aoinidh**. Just to the east of this clifftop there is a slope down to the undercliff on a reasonable gradient with deer tracks visibly descending the slope (NR489798).

On arriving on the undercliff platform, there are good views north to Ruantallain, north Jura and Colonsay and west to north-eastern Islay and the Rhuvaal Lighthouse. From here, work your way around Rubha Lang-aoinidh ('point of the long cliff') through the broken, rocky terrain beneath the cliff. After a few hundred metres, you will emerge onto a long bay with a beach of large cobbles. To the rear of the beach there are

deer tracks through the bracken, which make for easier walking.

At the end of this bay lies **Aird na Sgitheich** ('the hawthorn promontory') with an impressive collection of broken basalt dikes. Between here and Feolin Ferry you will encounter many such dikes with a south-east/north-west orientation (see the 'Geology' section above). Pass through the dikes onto another, longer bay with a broad beach of pebbles and rocky outcrops backed by an expanse of grass and bracken; again deer tracks will aid your passage. To the south-west, across the Sound of Islay, the small industrial complex of the Bunnahabhain distillery can be seen. ▶ Rather more prosaically, where **Allt na Gile** ('burn of the ravine') flows out to sea 1km south-west of Aird na Sgitheich, the wreckage of a small hovercraft can be found.

For the next 10km or so, this stretch of coastline is festooned with basalt dikes, rock arches, stacks, caves, waterfalls, raised beaches and other geological phenomena.

Shoreline at the western tip of south Loch Tarbert with Ruantallain in the background

A kilometre and a half beyond Allt na Gile, on the clifftop above Brein Phort, lies **Loch na Sgrioba** ('loch of the slide'). On the landward side of the loch, the terminus of the Sgriob na Caillich ('the old woman's slide') can be found. The 'slide' is a straight, 3km-long belt of angular boulders descending on a south-east–north-west orientation from 450m at the foot of Beinn an Oir to 30m above sea level. Regarded as one of the finest examples of a fossil medial moraine in the British Isles, the boulders were deposited between two convergent streams of the Devensian ice sheet that swept around and through the Paps from the east.

Map continued on page 82

This whole stretch of coastline is very interesting and once the undercliff has been gained back at Rubh' a' Chrois-aoinidh or Rubha Lang-aoinidh it is possible to walk as far as Rubha Bàrr nan Gobag along the shore depending on the tide. However, the undercliff route can be tough going in places – especially when carrying a heavy pack – with pebble beaches to be traversed, dikes to be scrambled over, around or through and a number of burns to cross. You may find yourself tempted to abandon the shoreline for an easier life and, in general, the going along the clifftops is reasonable; it isn't excessively tussocky, although it can be quite boggy in places.

Otherwise, keep to the shore until arriving at a large free-standing basalt dike 500m beyond **Rubha Aoineadh an Reithe** ('point of the cliff of the plain') where a worn path slopes up onto the clifftop (NR445746). A pair of obsolete telegraph poles should be visible to the south. If you quit the shore south-west of Rubha Aoinidh an Reithe, you will find that the terrain is quite level here – unsurprisingly given its name – but steer a course close to the cliff edge to avoid the worst of the boggy areas.

A kilometre further on, you will draw alongside **Loch a' Chnuic Bhric** ('loch of the speckled hill'), which is used for salmon farming. After another 1km you will have a fine view south across Traigh nam Feannag, the last of the magnificent raised beaches on the west coast walk. From the present shoreline, the beach rises more than 12m in a 'staircase' of 31 unvegetated shingle ridges, which are thought to indicate decreasing rates of glacio-isostatic uplift during the last 6000–7000 years of the Holocene. Whether you choose to descend to the shore here or steer a course above the beach, aim for the steps over the deer fence, which terminates at the lighthouse standing south-west of Traigh nam Feannag at **Carragh an t-Sruith** ('pillar of the tidal stream').

On crossing the fence, you will see **Inver Cottage** several hundred metres to the south-east, near the mouth of the Abhainn na h-Uanaire and a trio of lochans.

Map continued from
page 80

There are fine views of the Sound of
Islay, with the hills at that island's south-
eastern corner dominating the skyline.
Closer by, the Eilean Dhiura ferry can
be seen toing and froing between
Feolin and Port Askaig and 1km north
of Port Askaig there is the glazed and
whitewashed façade of the Caol Ila distillery, which announces its identity in
large black letters.

Pass around the back of Inver Cottage
by means of a gate in the deer fence and
pick up the track, which crosses the river
on a metal bridge, then follow the right hand
fork, heading south. Continue on this track as
it follows the shore along **Whitefarland Bay**
and when it climbs on to the low clifftop, you
have the choice of following it for an easier life or continuing along the shore. A further 1500m brings you to
Feolin Ferry and journey's end.

Waterfall on the Sound of Islay

Day 5 ALTERNATIVE
Glenbatrick Bay to the A846 via Glen Batrick

Distance	9km (5½ miles)
Time	3hrs
Start	Glenbatrick
	Grid ref: NR518800
Map	OS Explorer 355

This route is blessed with one of Jura's few footpaths, which is known as Evans' Walk and is named for Mr Henry Evans who established the Jura Forest deer hunting preserve in 1868. While Evans' Walk is a distinct path for much of its length there are sections that are difficult to follow; particularly the first few hundred metres and the last 1km before the road where it often disappears into the boggy terrain. The route also involves a fairly stiff 250m climb to the saddle between Beinn Tarsuinn and Corra Bheinn. From here, there is the option of undertaking a round of the Paps. On reaching the A846 road, Craighouse is a further 7km (4 miles). The Jura Bus calls at Three Arch Bridge – about 1km down the road – at 0732, 0918 and 1703 on schooldays and at 0914 and 1714 on Saturdays and school holidays.

Leaving Glenbatrick Bay, the path is picked up just to the rear of the house and heads directly south into **Glen Batrick** through a gap in the extinct cliff that stands at the mouth of the glen.

Just beyond the cliff, the path passes through the site of an **extinct lagoon** (NR518798), which served as a waterhole for Mesolithic and Neolithic encampments. An excavation of the site conducted by John Mercer in 1971–1972 turned up quantities of flint and quartzite tools and evidence of a cooking pit, which gave a radiocarbon date of 2950BC.

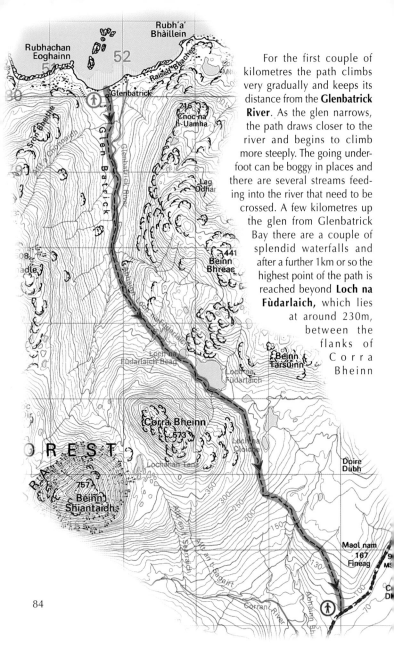

For the first couple of kilometres the path climbs very gradually and keeps its distance from the **Glenbatrick River**. As the glen narrows, the path draws closer to the river and begins to climb more steeply. The going underfoot can be boggy in places and there are several streams feeding into the river that need to be crossed. A few kilometres up the glen from Glenbatrick Bay there are a couple of splendid waterfalls and after a further 1km or so the highest point of the path is reached beyond **Loch na Fùdarlaich,** which lies at around 230m, between the flanks of Corra Bheinn ('steep peak') on its south-west side and Beinn Tarsuinn ('crossways peak') to the north-east.

If you're feeling strong and you have the time as well as reasonable weather, you might feel tempted to bag a Pap or two – or all three – as they loom above you. Such an endeavour would be best attempted by following the path south-east alongside Loch na Fùdarlaich as it contours around the flank of Corra Bheinn and then gradually bends a little further southwards, passing just west of three lochans. When you are directly west of the tip of the third of these lochans, **Loch na Cloiche** ('loch of the stone'), at around 220m, leave the path before it begins to drop and gradually climb around the flank of Corra Bheinn to the west. Once you're at 350m, contour around to the saddle between **Corra Bheinn** and **Beinn Shiantaidh**, which is dotted with a dozen or so lochans known collectively as the **Lochanan Tana**. A suggested itinerary for a round of the Paps is provided in Walk 2.

If you're saving the Paps for another time, continue to follow Evans' Walk south-east from Loch na Cloiche as it gradually drops down from the saddle between Corra Bheinn and Beinn Tarsuinn before bending sharply east and crossing a number of burns. The ground becomes considerably boggier here and the path is less distinct. However, you should be able to see the telegraph poles along the A846 by now, so if you continue heading south-east for 1km or so you'll reach the road with no problem.

Beinn an Oir and Beinn a' Chaolais (left) from the summit of Beinn Shiantaidh

WALK 2
Walking the Paps of Jura

Distance	17km (11 miles)
Time	6–8hrs
Start	A846 just over 1km north-east of Three Arch Bridge
	Grid ref: NR550732
Map	OS Explorer 355

A tour of all three Paps – Beinn Shiantaidh (pronounced Ben-a-Hinta), Beinn an Oir (Ben-an-Ore) and Beinn a' Chaolais (Ben-a-Hoolish) – makes for a big day's walk, involving 1500m (5000ft) of ascent and descent. From the summits of each of these mountains there are marvellous views to be had in fine weather, with Beinn an Oir benefiting from the most extensive. On a clear day, a 360° panorama takes in Scarba, Mull, the Garvellachs, Iona, Tiree and the Black Cuillin of Skye to the north; Colonsay and Oronsay to the north-west; Islay to the south-west, with the coast of Northern Ireland, Donegal and the Hills of Morne far beyond, and the hills of Arran visible beyond the Kintyre peninsula to the south-east.

Much of this route is without any form of path; the terrain is often boggy and tussocky and the scree-flanked mountainsides are extremely tough going in places. These mountains are very exposed and are best avoided in rough weather and poor visibility. A round of the Paps is no small endeavour and should only be attempted by those who are properly equipped and can read a map and use a compass. Always inform someone of your planned route and estimated time of completion.

The start of Evans' Walk is on the left-hand side of the A846, just over 1km north-east of Three Arch Bridge (NR550732). There is a lay-by on the opposite side of the road and a signpost, which points into the bog and indicates that this, as a concept at least, is Evans' Walk. The path is actually well defined for much of its length, though it can be difficult to follow in its early stages.

The eastern flank of Beinn Shiantaidh

From the signpost, climb north on a gentle gradient; there is sometimes a path of sorts along this first section, but this very much depends on usage and just how boggy the ground is at the time. After a few hundred metres the 'path' should bend to the north-west; if you avoid the temptation to climb too high on ATV tracks you're in with a good chance of finding yourself on Evans' Walk proper. Over the course of 1km, climb to around 150m then contour for a few hundred metres, crossing several burns in succession. Continue north-west, crossing another burn while climbing about 50m on a reasonable gradient, until you reach a rocky outcrop at around 200m (NR540747). The path should be more distinct by now, but you should abandon it as it bends to the north and continue north-west for another few hundred metres, climbing to about 250m around the flank of Corra Bheinn. From here, head west to 350m over the course of several hundred metres with **Beinn Shiantaidh** looming ever closer. On reaching 350m, contour around to the saddle between Corra Bheinn and Beinn Shiantaidh, with its dozen or more lochans known as the **Lochanan Tana** (NR525748).

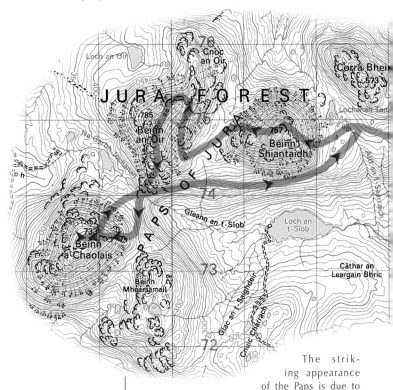

The striking appearance of the Paps is due to conical erosion occurring because of the lack of weaknesses and faults in the highly resistant quartzite rock. The quartzite scree blanketing the mountains' flanks was caused by the frost-shattering effects of the final cold period during the Lomond Re-advance (9300BC) after the ice had retreated from Jura at the end of the Devensian glacial period.

Paths of varying degrees of definition traverse each of the Paps, with Beinn an Oir benefiting from the best. The route up Beinn Shiantaidh is the toughest and the hardest to follow on account of its very steep scree slopes composed of large quartzite stones. There is a path of sorts which starts up the flank of the mountain to the south-east (NR502745), but this is soon subsumed into the scree. Intermittent patches of heather offer some respite from the ankle-jarring scree. A false summit is reached at 700m with the summit cairn a few hundred metres further west at 757m.

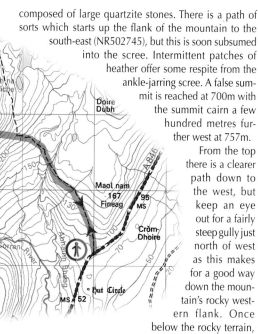

From the top there is a clearer path down to the west, but keep an eye out for a fairly steep gully just north of west as this makes for a good way down the mountain's rocky western flank. Once below the rocky terrain, head down the slope towards the saddle, making for the south-eastern flank of **Beinn an Oir** and the obvious path climbing south to north (NR503745).

This path makes for a surprisingly easy climb on an even gradient. After several hundred metres a narrower path heads more steeply north-west up onto the top ridge of the mountain. On gaining the ridge, swing south-west and continue along the last stretch to the top on a broad track levelled into the rocky terrain by Ordnance Survey mapmakers at the end of the 19th century. ▶

In 1764 the summit of Beinn an Oir was also used to conduct experiments to gauge the temperatures at which water boils at different altitudes.

At 785m or 2576ft Beinn an Oir is the highest of the Paps and the only one qualifying as a Corbett – those mountains between 2500 and 3000ft in Scotland (220) and in England and Wales (110). From the summit triangulation point (785m), descend the 400m to the saddle between this mountain and Beinn a' Chaolais by means

Beinn a' Chaolais and the largest of the Na-Garbh Lochanan from Beinn an Oir

of the southern spur, avoiding the very steep ground to your right. In good conditions there are great views onto **Beinn a' Chaolais** with Islay and its eponymous sound beyond. There are reasonable paths to assist your descent, which becomes a scree slope on its final stretch.

The saddle is gained at 370m, just above the uppermost of the **Na Garbh-lochanan** (NR495741). Walk towards the saddle between the eastern flank of Beinn a' Chaolais and **Beinn Mhearsamail**, gaining around 30m. From around NR494734, climb directly west up the eastern spur and arrive at the summit 330m above the saddle (733m). Initially descend by the same route, but look out for tracks descending the steep scree slopes north-east to the Na Garbh-lochanan saddle. From the saddle, contour beneath the southern flanks of Beinn an Oir and Beinn Shiantaidh at around 350m and retrace your steps to the Evans' Walk path and back to the A846.

Alternative return routes from Beinn a' Chaolais include descending to Keils by way of Gleann Astaile and the Abhainn a' Mhinisteir, which can be boggy and difficult to navigate in poor visibility. Contouring around the southern side of Gleann an t-Siob above Loch an t-Siob and the Corran River to Three Arch Bridge presents no navigational difficulties and is furnished with ATV tracks for some of the way, but it can be horrendously boggy at times. This is a route that I'd recommend after a period of dry weather only.

WALK 3
Evans' Walk to Glenbatrick Bay, Feolin Ferry or the head of Loch Tarbert

Distance	to Glenbatrick Bay and back: 18km (11 miles) to Feolin Ferry and back: 25km (15½ miles) to head of Loch Tarbert and back: 18km (11 miles)
Time	to Glenbatrick Bay: 6hrs to Feolin Ferry: 8–10hrs to head of the loch: 7–8hrs
Start	Left-hand side of the A846, just over 1km north-east of Three Arch Bridge Grid ref: NR550732
Map	OS Explorer 355
Note	If intending to walk this route during the deer stalking season, contact the head keeper of the Tarbert Estate in advance on (01496) 820207

Although Evans' Walk is blessed with one of Jura's few 'paths', the path itself can tend to disappear into the boggy ground at each end of the route, near the A846 and Glenbatrick Bay respectively. Once on the path proper it is easy enough to follow over the saddle between Corra Bheinn and Beinn Tarsuinn. In clear weather you will enjoy wonderful views of the Paps and across Loch Tarbert to the wild fastness of north Jura as you descend into Glen Batrick. The return involves a fairly tough climb to the saddle beyond Loch na Fùdarlaich.

The Jura Bus leaves Craighouse for Three Arch Bridge at 0720, 0808, 1550 and 1635 on schooldays and at 0808 and 1550 on Saturdays and school holidays (including Sundays). For the return journey, the bus calls at Three Arch Bridge en route to Craighouse at 1703 on schooldays and 1714 on Saturdays and school holidays.

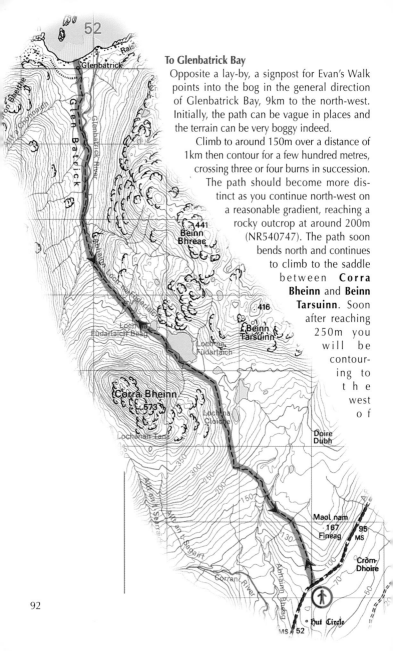

To Glenbatrick Bay

Opposite a lay-by, a signpost for Evan's Walk points into the bog in the general direction of Glenbatrick Bay, 9km to the north-west. Initially, the path can be vague in places and the terrain can be very boggy indeed.

Climb to around 150m over a distance of 1km then contour for a few hundred metres, crossing three or four burns in succession. The path should become more distinct as you continue north-west on a reasonable gradient, reaching a rocky outcrop at around 200m (NR540747). The path soon bends north and continues to climb to the saddle between **Corra Bheinn** and **Beinn Tarsuinn**. Soon after reaching 250m you will be contouring to the west of

Loch na Cloiche and two other sizeable lochans, before the path bends north-west again and follows the shore of **Loch na Fùdarlaich**.

Loch na Fùdarlaich

The path soon begins its descent into **Glen Batrick** alongside the **Abhainn Loch na Fùdarlaich**, which tumbles into the glen in a series of whisky-hued cascades. The path keeps to the left bank of the river for most of its length, with the exception of a couple fords in its lower reaches. Further down the glen, the river is fed by a number of burns flowing off the surrounding hills and at its confluence with the Allt Teanga nan Abhainn it becomes the **Glenbatrick River**. None of these burns is difficult to cross, though the lower reaches of the glen can be very boggy.

When you near **Glenbatrick Bay**, the path leads you down through the ramparts of an extinct cliff and delivers you to the rear of Glenbatrick Lodge – a finer location for a 'summer house' is hard to imagine. If the weather is clement, a swim – for the robust – and picnic on the beautiful beach can be enjoyed. Before heading back, it is worth having a look at the massive raised beach that lies above the western end of the bay – just follow the obvious ATV tracks to the end of the bay and up a short incline.

To return to the A846, just retrace your steps.

The Sound of Islay

To Feolin Ferry

Another option is to continue on from Glenbatrick Bay to Feolin Ferry around the coast, although this makes for a long and demanding day's walk. The total distance from the start of Evans' Walk to Feolin is approximately 25km (15½ miles) and will take 8–10hrs. For a description of the onward route from Glenbatrick Bay, see Walk 1 Day 5. This route can of course be walked in either direction, but Evan's Walk is arguably the tougher section of the walk

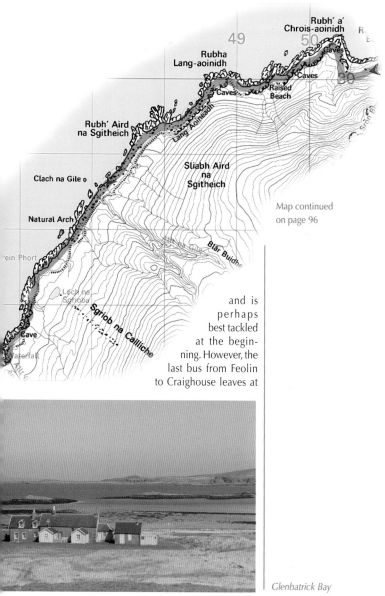

49

Rubh' a'
Chrois-aoinidh

50

Caves

Rubha
Lang-aoinidh

Caves

Caves

Raised
Beach

Rubh' Aird
na Sgitheich

Lang Aoineadh

Clach na Gile

Sliabh Aird
na
Sgitheich

Map continued
on page 96

Natural Arch

Blàr Buidhe

'ein Phort

and is
perhaps
best tackled
at the begin-
ning. However, the
last bus from Feolin
to Craighouse leaves at

Loch na
Sgrioba

Sgrìob na Cailliche

Cave

Waterfall

Glenbatrick Bay

Map continued
from page 95

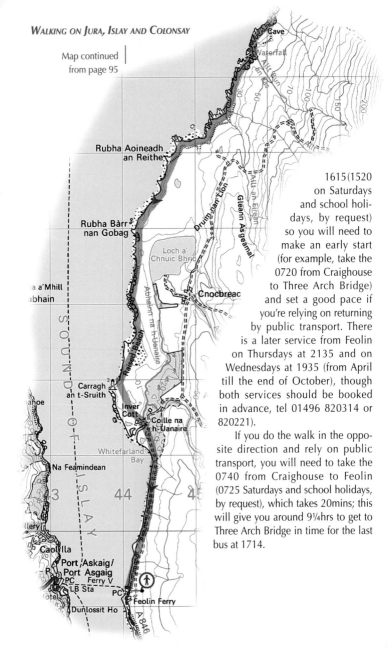

1615 (1520 on Saturdays and school holidays, by request) so you will need to make an early start (for example, take the 0720 from Craighouse to Three Arch Bridge) and set a good pace if you're relying on returning by public transport. There is a later service from Feolin on Thursdays at 2135 and on Wednesdays at 1935 (from April till the end of October), though both services should be booked in advance, tel 01496 820314 or 820221).

If you do the walk in the opposite direction and rely on public transport, you will need to take the 0740 from Craighouse to Feolin (0725 Saturdays and school holidays, by request), which takes 20mins; this will give you around 9¼hrs to get to Three Arch Bridge in time for the last bus at 1714.

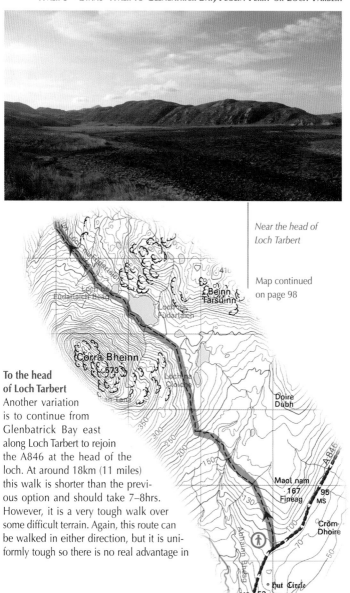

*Near the head of
Loch Tarbert*

Map continued
on page 98

**To the head
of Loch Tarbert**

Another variation
is to continue from
Glenbatrick Bay east
along Loch Tarbert to rejoin
the A846 at the head of the
loch. At around 18km (11 miles)
this walk is shorter than the previous option and should take 7–8hrs.
However, it is a very tough walk over
some difficult terrain. Again, this route can
be walked in either direction, but it is uni-
formly tough so there is no real advantage in

Map continued
from page 97

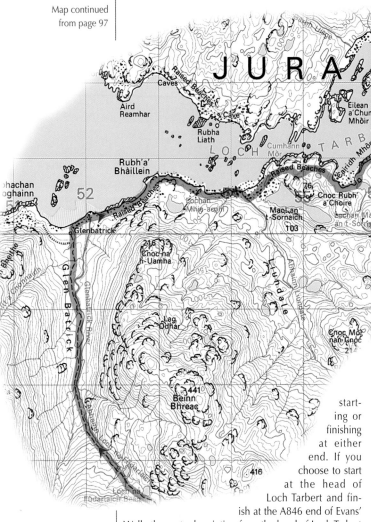

starting or finishing at either end. If you choose to start at the head of Loch Tarbert and finish at the A846 end of Evans' Walk, the route description from the head of Loch Tarbert to Glenbatrick Bay is included in Walk 1 Day 4. If you

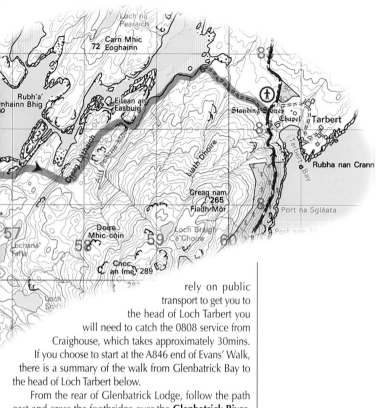

rely on public
transport to get you to
the head of Loch Tarbert you
will need to catch the 0808 service from
Craighouse, which takes approximately 30mins.
If you choose to start at the A846 end of Evans' Walk,
there is a summary of the walk from Glenbatrick Bay to
the head of Loch Tarbert below.

From the rear of Glenbatrick Lodge, follow the path
east and cross the footbridge over the **Glenbatrick River**.
Follow the path down towards the shore and follow the
ATV tracks heading east as far as the small sandy beach
just before **Rubh' a' Bhàillien**. Pick your way around the
point through broken dikes and rocky terrain, then cross
several pebble beaches intersected by rocky outcrops
until you arrive at the **Abhainn Luindale**. Cross the river
and make your way across the massive pebble bank of
Maol an t-Sornaich. Once across, look for paths up on
to higher ground to the west and steer a course north
of a small lochan (NR552807) beneath **Cnoc Rubh' a'
Choire**. Follow the obvious deer tracks down to the small
bay at **Cairidh Mhor** where there is a dammed lochan.
The dam can be walked across with care in dry weather;

*Lochan Maol an
t-Sornaich*

alternatively, walk around the lochan to be on the safe side. Continue north-east, following the shore on level ground for around 1.5km. A couple of hundred metres beyond Sgeir na Muic-mara, look for a route up a shallow, but boggy gully (NR568814). Skirt the flank of a small hill, crossing a burn and then contour just north of east along a small ridge for a couple of hundred metres. Cross an area of boggy open ground to the east and make for the steep flank of **Creag Làthaic** (NR576814), keeping south of a U-shaped bay. Find a route up onto the ridge and look out for deer tracks heading north-east along the western side of the ridge; follow these for around 1km, gaining and losing a little height here and there until you arrive at a small gap in the ridge at NR586820. Follow the tracks through the gap and drop down to Bàgh an Uillt Fhearna. There are stepping stones across the burn running into the bay from the south; cross here and continue around the shoreline for 1km until you arrive at a **boathouse** with a small jetty. From here, follow the track road, which bends south-east and reaches the **A846** after a 1km.

From Monday to Saturday the Jura Bus passes Tarbert at around 1700, though it is best to be there in advance and times should be checked with the Jura Bus Company, tel 01496 820314 or 01496 820221).

ISLAY

Port Domhnuill Chruinn, north-west Islay

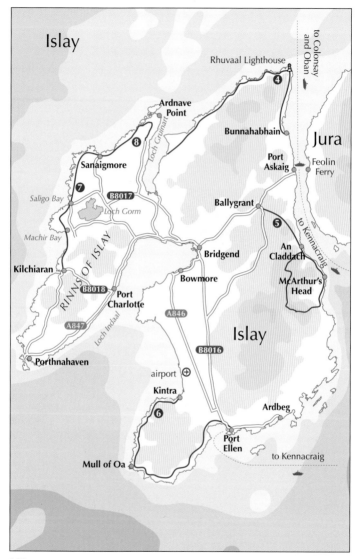

Islay

Rhuvaal Lighthouse

to Colonsay
and Oban

4

Ardnave
Point

Bunnahabhain

Jura

8

Loch Gruinart

Port
Askaig

Feolin
Ferry

Sanaigmore

7

B8017

Ballygrant

5

An
Claddach

Saligo Bay

Loch Gorm

to Kennacraig

Machir Bay

RINNS OF ISLAY

Bridgend

McArthur's
Head

Kilchiaran

B8018

Port
Charlotte

Bowmore

A847

Loch Indaal

A846

Islay

B8016

Porthnahaven

airport

Kintra

6

Ardbeg

Mull of Oa

Port
Ellen

to Kennacraig

INTRODUCTION

Walking to An Claddach along the Sound of Islay (Walk 5)

Islay (Scottish Gaelic: *Ìle*), pronounced eye-la, is the southernmost of the Inner Hebrides and lies at the entrance of the Firth of Lorn, some 40km (25 miles) north of the Irish coast and 20km (12½ miles) west of the Kintyre peninsula. Colonsay is 9km to the north and Jura lies 1km to the east across the Sound of Islay. There is a marked contrast between Islay and her rugged, mountainous neighbour; much of the island is low-lying and fertile, hence agriculture and land management are major influences on the landscape. However, Islay has a varied terrain that also includes rugged quartzite uplands – moorland, hills (the highest being Beinn Bheigeir

at 491m) and high sea cliffs – as well as extensive areas of heathland, blanket bog, marshland, sand flats, dunes, machair and raised beach deposits. The island is 40km (25 miles) in length from north to south and 25km (15½ miles) from east to west at its widest point. Two sea lochs, Loch Gruinart to the north and Loch Indaal to the south, all but separate the western Rinns of Islay (sometimes spelt 'Rhinns') from the rest of the island – and probably once did.

The landscape of Islay is awash with history; the coastline is dotted with Iron Age forts, or 'duns', and poignant monuments attest to the many lives lost in shipwrecks along

Islay's coast. The hinterland is also scattered with the ruins and traces of settlements – ancient and recent – and those of ancient and modern conflicts. The island has a long history of human occupation, but today's population of 3500 is a quarter of its pre-clearance peak of 15,000 in the 1830s.

However, Islay is very much a thriving island community today and there is a tangible air of industry about the place. Islay's economy is in comparatively good shape, partly due to the growth of the international market for the island's eight brands of single malt whisky. The distilleries themselves are a magnet for enthusiasts and other visitors. The flourishing tourist industry is also a mainstay of the local economy, with freshwater fishing, bird watching and golf being the other major attractions. Agriculture, fishing, forestry and deer stalking are the other main industries on the island.

HISTORY

Finds of tools, shell middens and structural remains dating from the Mesolithic period, show that Islay was first occupied by nomadic hunter-gatherers as early as 8000BC; following the retreat of the ice cap at the end of the last glacial period. However, harsh winters probably limited settlement during this period to the seasonal exploitation of the island's natural resources.

By the early sixth millenium BC, as the climate improved, hunter-gatherers throughout the region began settling in agriculture-based communities. The fertile land of Islay attracted these early farmers and there is widespread evidence of Neolithic (4000–2000BC) occupation throughout the island, including chambered burial cairns and settlement sites.

Archaeological research and chance finds have uncovered traces from the Bronze Age (c2500-600BC) and Iron Age (c600BC–AD400), but as yet little is known about the lives of Islay's inhabitants during these periods. There are a number of fortified 'dun' sites throughout the island, including many along the coast, but the period of their construction and use is unclear, although some probably date from the Iron Age.

Dál Riata

By the early Middle Ages, the Inner Hebrides and the Kintyre peninsula had been colonised by tribes from the north of Ireland, thus becoming part of the kingdom of Dál Riata. Islay was ruled by the Cenél nÓengusa, one of three kin groups forming the kingdom in what is present-day Argyll. During this period, Christianity came to Islay and the legacy of St Columba's missionaries is visible around the island in the remains of many chapels, such as those of Kilchiaran and Kilslevan, and later carved stone crosses like those in the burial grounds at Kildalton and Kilnave. The Christian influence is also evident in the frequent appearance of the prefix 'Kil' – originating from the

Gaelic *cill*, meaning 'church' – in Islay place names.

Towards the end of the eighth century, Vikings arrived in the Inner Hebrides; initially they came as raiders, plundering monasteries and terrorising the indigenous populations, then later as traders and settlers when Islay became an important staging post between Scandinavia and Viking colonies in Ireland and the Isle of Man. The Norse settlers intermarried with the indigenous population and became known as the Gael-Gall. Apart from a few pagan burial sites, few traces of Norse settlements have been found on Islay, although there are a number of Norse place names on the island.

Clan Donald

In 1156, Norse ascendancy in the region was checked by the emergence of Somerled, a powerful figure of mixed Gaelic-Norse ancestry. He took advantage of the death of King Olaf of Man to invade the Southern Hebrides and establish himself as ruler, dividing the Norse Kingdom of Man and the Isles in the process. Somerled consolidated his power with campaigns in Ireland and against the King of Scotland. He was succeeded by his son Ranald, who named himself King of the Isles and Lord of Argyll. Ranald's son Donald inherited the kingdom of Islay and founded the Clan Donald.

After defeat in battle to the Scots, Clan Donald ceded rule of the isles to the Scottish Crown in 1266. However, after supporting Robert the Bruce in the Scottish Wars of Independence early in the 14th century, the MacDonalds under Angus Òg, a descendant of Somerled, had their forfeited lands restored. Under Angus's son John, the MacDonalds re-established themselves as the Lords of the Isles. The Lords of the Isles ruled their domain from Finlaggan on Islay for more than 150 years, until the exposure of John MacDonald II's treasonous treaty with Edward IV of England against the Scottish Crown. The MacDonald's lands were forfeit in 1493 following John's defeat in battle by James IV.

After the fall of John MacDonald II, a period of rebellions ensued until James IV returned lands on Islay to John of Ardnamurchan, a MacDonald. On his death, administration of the island's estates was initially overseen by Sir John Campbell of Cawdor and subsequently by the Earl of Argyll, until much of the land came under the control of King James V in 1542. Donald Dubh of Clan Donald then attempted to restore the lordship by force, but the rebellion failed when he died at Drogheda in 1545. However, hostilities over control of Islay's lands continued and in 1598 the MacDonalds and MacLeans fought the Battle of Loch Gruinart over ownership of the Rinns of Islay. The MacDonalds were victorious on this occasion.

The Campbells

The downfall of the MacDonalds presaged the rise of the Campbells, who ruled Islay as agents of the Crown. The Campbells increased their land holdings and influence on the island, but they were absentee lairds and for much of the 17th century Islay's fortunes were allowed to decline. By the early 18th century, the Cawdor Campbells were obliged to sell their estates on Islay to Daniel Campbell of Shawfield. Campbell and his successors, Daniel the Younger and Walter Campbell, did much to improve circumstances on the island, improving farming methods, introducing linen production, developing a fishing industry and building the village of Bowmore along with schools, roads and quays.

By the time Walter Frederick Campbell became laird in 1816, the population of Islay had grown exponentially, despite emigration to the New World. In order to meet the needs of population growth, Campbell built the villages of Port Ellen, Port Charlotte and Port Wemyss and engaged in widespread land improvement, promoting smallholdings and land reclamation, as well as the development of the distilling industry. However, emigration continued apace and by the 1840s, the potato famine precipitated an exodus. By 1848, Campbell was bankrupt, with his lands sequestered and administered on behalf of his creditors. In the ensuing period, the population was subjected to land clearances. In 1853, the Islay estates were split up and sold off to private individuals, many of whom were absentee landlords unconcerned with the improvement of the island or

Looking down on Port an Eas, south-west of Port Ellen (Walk 6)

A rock arch seen through another rock arch, north-west Islay

the circumstances of its population. Much of Islay remains in the ownership of a few individuals today.

Islay's fortunes have greatly improved in recent years, however, and the population is slowly growing again. The success of the whisky distilling industry and the growth of tourism have greatly supplemented the island's income from agriculture and the fishing industry. Improved transport links with the mainland can only enhance Islay's economic development.

GEOLOGY

Islay's notably varied geological composition results from exposure to diverse and periodically extreme climates and environments that have shaped the island over the course of millions of years. Sedimentary rocks such as sandstone, limestone and shale predominate. Most sediments have been exposed to some degree of heat and pressure, metamorphosing them to quartzite, psammite, phylitte and slate. These rocks are Precambrian (c1000-600 million years old) and belong to the Dalradian Supergroup and the Colonsay and Bowmore Groups.

Islay's rocks are not all of sedimentary origin, however. The southern end of the Rinns of Islay – the western part of the island, which is almost separated from the rest of Islay by Loch Gruinart and Loch Indaal – is composed of igneous rock that has undergone numerous phases of folding and metamorphism. These Palaeo-proterozoic (c1800 million years old) gneisses, which are the oldest rock in Europe, form the basement rock onto which Colonsay Group sediments were deposited. The rock is known as the Rinns Complex, which was formerly believed to be part of the Lewisian Gneiss Complex forming the Outer Hebrides.

Islay has many folds, faults and shear zones; the most significant is the Loch Gruinart Fault, which is a branch of the Great Glen Fault. Erosion along this fault line resulted in the formation of the island's two sea lochs. It is thought that a tidal strait connected the lochs between 8000 and 2000 years ago. South-east of the Loch Gruinart Fault the rocks are structurally dominated by a major fold known as the Islay Anticline. In common with the rest of Scotland, most of the island's structural features were formed by the collision of two tectonic plates 500–400 million years ago. During the Mesozoic period (c265–245 million years ago), Islay was part of a desert that was subsequently submerged by a shallow sea. Sediments formed during this period are visible as red breccia and sandstone along the southern coast of the Mull of Oa.

Around 65 million years ago, during the Lower Tertiary period, the west coast of Scotland was subject to intense volcanic activity during the formation of the Atlantic Ocean. There were no volcanoes on Islay, but numerous dikes were formed when upwelling magma filled cracks in the Earth's crust radiating out from centres of eruption on Arran and Mull. Today, these dikes are most apparent along sections of the island's coast where erosion of the country rock into which they are intruded has left them exposed as natural walls.

During the last glacial period (c75,000-12,000bc) of the current Ice Age, Islay was covered by the ice sheet flowing south-westwards over the islands from the centre of the ice cap in the area of Rannoch Moor. The passage of the ice sheet locked up fresh water and ground and smoothed the rock with the characteristic east-west striations caused by glacier-borne stones. When the ice sheet receded, extensive deposits of sand, gravel, till and boulders were left behind. The weight of the ice cap had also depressed the landmass and when it melted the sea level rose and the land gradually rebounded. This process, described as 'glacio-isostatic uplift', continued long after the sea level reached its maximum, resulting in the exposure of raised beaches and formerly submarine caves, rock arches and stacks. These phenomena are most prevalent along Islay's north-west coast and around the Oa peninsula.

WILDLIFE
Islay's diverse terrain provides habitats for a rich variety of wildlife and the island's large tracts of undeveloped land together with sensitive land management have allowed many species to thrive. Islay's wildlife is prolific,

and enthusiasts visiting the island to observe species in their natural habitats are unlikely to be disappointed.

Islay has a population of several thousand red deer, mainly distributed through the hills of the north and east, although there are about 100 on the Rinns around the Loch Gruinart RSPB reserve. Roe deer are common on low ground and in the forestry plantations. Fallow deer are found in the south-east of the island where there is a sizeable population. There are several hundred wild goats on Islay, with population concentrations around the Oa peninsula and around the north and west coasts. Otters are common around Islay's coast though shy and not always the easiest animals to spot. Patient observation on quiet stretches of coast is the best approach.

The brown hare is widespread and common in some areas; groups of 20 or more can sometimes be seen in spring. Rabbits are prolific; black and parti-coloured animals can sometimes be spotted in the island's dune warrens. The house mouse, wood mouse, brown rat, water shrew, pygmy shrew and common shrew are all fairly widespread on the island, the latter – *Sorex araneus granti* – being a distinct race from mainland shrews. The field or short-tailed vole

found on the island belongs to a separate Islay race – *Microtus agrestis fiona* – which is common and widespread. The Islay stoat – *Mustela erminea ricinae* – has been posited as a separate race on account of its smaller size and head measurements, though this is not widely accepted.

The common long-eared bat is the only common large bat found on Islay. The pipistrelle and Naterrer's bat are present, though not common. Escaped mink have appeared in recent years, having made the crossing from the mainland. Domestic ferrets have escaped into the wild and are well established around rabbit warrens. Hedgehogs were illicitly introduced during the 1950s and 1970s – they are widespread and common. Feral cats are found in some areas, especially around rabbit warrens, though these are not the distinct species of Scottish wild cat – *Felis sylvestris grampia*.

There is a population of several hundred common seals around

Atlantic grey seal pup

the coasts, concentrated along the south-east coastline and on the skerries (rocky islands) south of Bowmore on Loch Indaal. Grey seals breed on Nave Island off Ardnave Point and can be seen hauled out on the sandbanks of Loch Gruinart. They are also present on the islands of Orsay and Eilean Mhic Coinnich off Portnahaven at the southern tip of the Rinns. They are often seen in the harbour at Portnahaven.

Minke whales, pilot whales, killer whales, porpoises and white-beaked, common, Risso's and bottle-nosed dolphins are sometimes seen close inshore. The latter is the most common, frequently coming right in to Port Ellen Bay and Loch Indaal. Dead specimens of sperm, minke and pilot whales have all been washed ashore on Islay in recent years.

The adder is the only snake occurring on Islay; it is widely distributed, although numbers have declined in recent years. The common lizard is found throughout Islay, but is not common. The common frog and common toad are widespread and common. It is thought that the great crested newt may be present on the island.

Islay is probably most renowned for its diverse and spectacular birdlife. More than 200 species can be seen, of which almost 100 breed on the island. The approach of winter brings almost 50,000 migrating white-fronted and barnacle geese from Greenland and Canada. From October to April, huge numbers of these birds can be seen

roosting at Loch Gruinart and in the fields around Bridgend or taking to the air each morning. Canada, Brent and pinkfoot geese also winter on the island. Resident and migratory ducks include the wigeon, red-breasted merganser, eider, teal, shoveler, goldeneye, pochard and scaup.

The island's resident raptors include the merlin, peregrine, kestrel, sparrowhawk, hen harrier, buzzard, golden eagle, barn owl, tawny owl and short-eared owl. Ospreys visit on passage, occasional red kites winter or pass through and vagrant goshawks, gyr falcons, marsh harriers and white-tailed eagles are seen infrequently.

There are many seabirds resident on Islay and a good number of wintering or passing birds as well, including common, black-headed, great black-backed, herring and Iceland gulls, fulmars, kittiwakes, storm petrels, manx shearwaters, common, little and arctic terns, cormorants, shags, gannets, guillemots and razorbills.

The rare chough can be seen around the island, although the Oa, Ardnave and the Rinns are the places you are most likely to spot it. Lapwings, curlews and corncrakes can be seen – or more likely heard in the latter case – around the island's farmlands and the Loch Gruinart nature reserve. Other wading birds seen around Loch Gruinart include the turnstone, dunlin, oystercatcher, godwit, redshank, snipe and sanderling. The little, great-crested and scarce Slavonian grebes and the red-throated, black-throated and great northern divers can be seen on Islay's freshwater and sea lochs and along some stretches of the coast. The grey heron, mute and whooper swan also haunt the island's lochs, coastline and rivers.

FLOWERS AND PLANTS

Islay's diverse geology, temperate climate and land use result in a varied terrain that includes grazed pasture and arable farmland, rugged quartzite uplands and hill country, woodlands, heathland, marshland, moorland, blanket bog, vegetated raised beach deposits and sea cliffs, sand dune systems, coastal grasslands and machair, sand flats and salt-marsh. These diverse habitats are home to a wide range of vegetation including more than 900 flowering plants.

Islay's heathland is dominated by ericaceous dwarf shrubs such as bell heather and bilberry as well as gorse; areas of bog, marsh and fen sustain a variety of plants including black bog-rush, white beak-sedge, bog myrtle, bog asphodel, sundews, mosses, bog cotton, meadow thistle, rushes, marsh arrowgrass, marsh cinquefoil, pale butterwort, fairy flax and a variety of orchids. Sea pinks, orchids, primrose and centaurium cling to an existence along the coastal margins. A walk along Islay's bracken-fringed country roads can reveal a riotous tangle of wild flowers, including goldenrod, astilbe, daisies, foxglove, Queen Anne's lace, ragged robin, wild gooseberies, flag iris, purple thistle and wild fuscia.

Areas of coastal 'machair' – a type of fertile, low-lying sand dune pasture – such as those occurring along the west coast of the Rinns, burst into bloom in May and build to a floral climax in July. Endemic species include the buttercup, bird's foot trefoil, saxifrages and carline thistle, scarlet pimpernel, eyebright, thyme, clover, wild pansy, violets, daisy, harebell, silverweed and hawkbit, mountain everlasting, gentians and orchids.

There are extensive areas of coniferous plantation on the Rinns, the Oa, south-east of Bowmore, north of Finlaggan and west of Bunnahabain. There are also sizeable mixed deciduous/coniferous plantations around Bridgend, Ballygrant, south of Port Askaig and around Kildalton. Species include Douglas, noble and European silver fir, Norway and Sitka spruce, lodgepole, Corsican and Scots pine,

Sea pinks

European larch, Japanese red-cedar, yew, beech, silver birch, sweet chestnut and evergreen oak. Areas of indigenous woodland – including species such as birch, sessile oak, hazel, willow and rowan – can be found in small pockets around the island, especially parts of the east and southeast coasts. The deciduous woodland provides a habitat for ferns, mosses, lichens and liverworts and in spring the woodland floor is covered with snowdrops, wild daffodils, bluebells, violets and primroses.

Dense bracken, bell heather and bog myrtle cover is widespread in uninhabited, un-farmed coastal and upland areas and can hinder walkers.

GETTING AROUND

In contrast to Jura and Colonsay, there is a fairly extensive network of roads on Islay, including A-roads, B-roads and single-track country roads, which give access to most points on the island. The bus service operated by Islay Coaches (tel 01496 840273) services two routes:

- Service 450 runs from Portnahaven to Ardbeg via Bridgend and Bowmore
- Service 451 runs from Port Askaig to Ardbeg via Bridgend and Bowmore

These services are essentially designed to connect with ferry and plane arrivals and to connect the various settlements with Bowmore, the island's capital. While the bus services are of some use for walkers, routes to

the north coast of Islay – and some of the island's finest walking – are not serviced. The Islay bus timetable is full of Byzantine permutations, which there is no space to untangle here. Copies of the bus timetable are available from the Tourist Office in Bowmore, tel 01496 810254, or online at www.argyll-bute.gov.uk.

Taking your own car is another option, but is of limited use for linear walks. There are a number of taxis on the island and some of these are listed in Appendix B.

Suggestions are also given for getting to and from each of the walks.

WHEN TO GO

Islay is a wonderful place to visit at any time of year. The climate is relatively mild, thanks to the Gulf Stream, hence temperatures seldom drop below zero in winter and 16°C is the daily maximum average during the warmest months of July and August. April, May and June are the sunniest and driest months and midsummer benefits from 18 hours of daylight. The autumn months can vary tremendously, from gales and heavy showers to bright sunshine in quick succession. Fast-moving bands of rain interspersed with sunshine make rainbows a frequent phenomenon. Rainfall increases in the autumn, with October through to January being the wettest months. Daylight hours decrease from 12 in late September to seven in late November. Because of the mild climate and the island's generally low-

Port Ghill Greamhair, north-west of Sanaigmore

lying disposition, it seldom snows on Islay, but the island is frequently battered by winter storms raging in off the Atlantic. Therefore, the winter months are better suited to shorter walks along the island's many beautiful sandy bays – especially those along the west coast. Winter storms battering the Atlantic coast are wonderful to behold from a place of safety or if an easy and clear line of retreat is available. In summary, spring, summer and autumn are the best seasons for undertaking the challenging coastal and hill walks described below.

Islay has become increasingly popular during the summer months in recent years, but beyond the island's many lovely beaches, walkers will encounter few other people along the wilder stretches of coastline or out among the hills. However, accommodation can be over-subscribed at the height of the season and at other times

of year such as Hogamanay or during the Islay Jazz Festival in September.

Like almost everywhere in the Highlands and Islands, Islay is not immune from midges during the summer, although they seldom seem as intense as those on Jura. Bracken cover can also be a drawback for walkers during the summer.

ACCOMMODATION
There is a wide range of self-catering, bed and breakfast, hotel and guest house accommodation on the island, as well as a SYHA hostel at Port Charlotte and two campsites. An important consideration when choosing where to stay is the location in relation to your intended walks. Bowmore is central and the hub of transport and amenities, so is an obvious choice if you're staying a while and walking in different parts of the island. With a population of around

113

1000, Bowmore is hardly a metropolis; however, if you prefer something quieter, Port Charlotte on the opposite shore of Loch Indaal is a fine place to stay. As well as its magnificent views, it is on the 450 bus route and also has a number of amenities (see below) including the excellent Port Mòr campsite, the youth hostel, two hotels with bars and restaurants and two cafés. Accommodation also includes bed and breakfast and self-catering options. If you prefer quieter still, self-catering and bed and breakfast accommodation is scattered all over the island and wild camping is also possible. A small selection of accommodation is listed in Appendix A. More comprehensive lists are available from the Tourist Office in Bowmore, tel 01496 810254, or online at www.islayinfo.com.

The **SYHA hostel** in Port Charlotte is a large, whitewashed former whisky bond situated on Main Street. It is a well-equipped and comfortable hostel with 30 beds. It is open between the beginning of April and end of September – dates vary each year. Telephone 01496 850385; online bookings at www.syha.org.uk.

There are also two excellent campsites on Islay. **Port Mòr** is just outside Port Charlotte on the Portnahaven road and is open all year round for tents and camper vans. The site overlooks Loch Indaal and has showers, toilets, laundry facilities, café and wireless internet, tel 01496 850411. **Kintra Farm** is 5km from Port

Ellen and its campsite is set amid sand dunes next to the long sandy strand of Laggan Bay, looking out across Loch Indaal to the Rinns of Islay. The site has toilets and showers; tel 01496 302051 or email margaretanne@kintrafarm.co.uk.

There are many excellent sites for **wild camping** on Islay, which is permitted in accordance with the Land Reform (Scotland) Act 2003. However, camping is restricted to areas where access rights are exercisable. The Scottish Outdoor Access Code (see the 'Accommodation' section for Jura) spells out a camper's responsibilities, which are only common sense. In addition to these general considerations, it is important to avoid bird nesting areas.

AMENITIES

There are three **banks** on Islay, two in Bowmore and one in Port Ellen, and they each have cash points. Bowmore has the island's only sizeable **supermarket**, which also has the longest opening hours. There are general grocery shops in Port Ellen, Bridgend, Bruichladdich, Port Charlotte and smaller newsagent/shops in Port Askaig, Ballygrant and Portnahaven. There are **petrol stations** in Port Askaig, Bridgend, Port Charlotte, Bowmore and Port Ellen.

The **Islay Hospital** is in Bowmore, tel 01496 301000. **The Rhinns Medical Centre** is in Port Charlotte, tel 01496 850210. **The Surgery** GP practice is in Bowmore, tel 01496 810273. The

Islay Pharmacy is on Bowmore's Main Street. The local police station is in Bowmore, tel 01496 810222.

Bowmore Post Office is near the top of Main Street. Port Ellen Post Office is at 66 Frederick Crescent. There are also post offices in or near the stores in Ballygrant, Portnahaven, Port Charlotte, Bridgend and Bruichladdich.

The Wildlife Information Centre, run by The Islay Natural History Trust, is situated in the same building as the youth hostel in Port Charlotte and is well worth a visit, tel 01496 850288. The award-winning Museum of Islay Life is also found in Port Charlotte and is a fascinating repository of artefacts and personal correspondence that chart the island's history from ancient times to the present day, tel 01496 850358.

FOOD AND DRINK

There are a number of excellent places to eat on Islay. One of the best is the Port Charlotte Hotel where the emphasis is on local produce. The restaurant is not cheap, but it's good value and there is a more affordable bar menu. Similarly, the Harbour Inn is not cheap, but offers excellent value for quality food. Staying upmarket, the restaurant at the An Tigh-Osda hotel in Bruichladdich is also well regarded. Food is served at other hotels and pubs, including the Lochside Hotel in Bowmore; An Tighe Seinsse in Portnahaven; the Brigend Hotel; the Ballygrant Inn and Restaurant; The White Hart Hotel in Port Ellen; the Port Askaig Hotel and the Lochindaal Hotel in Port Charlotte. There are two Indian restaurants: The Maharani Restaurant in Port Ellen and the Taj Mahal in Bowmore.

Tea rooms, cafés and restaurants with daytime opening include: The Croft Kitchen and the Port Mòr Centre in Port Charlotte; The Cottage Restaurant in Bowmore; the Mactaggart Cybercafe in Port Ellen and The Old Kiln Café at the Ardbeg Distillery, outside Port Ellen; the Kilchoman Distillery café at Kilchoman near Machair Bay.

There are eight distilleries on the island, all of which run regular tours, though some by appointment only. Even if you're teetotal or can't stand whisky, a distillery tour is a fascinating experience.

Laphroaig tel 01496 302418, www.laphroaig.com

Lagavulin tel 01496 302730

Ardbeg tel 01496 302244, www.ardbeg.com

Bowmore tel 01496 810441, www.bowmore.co.uk

Bruichladdich tel 01496 850190, www.bruichladdich.com

Kilchoman tel 01496 850011, www.kilchomandistillery.com

Caol Ila tel 01496 302760

Bunnahabhain tel 01496 840646, www.bunnahabhain.com

WALK 4
Bunnahabhain to Killinallan

Distance	25km (15½ miles)
Time	7–8hrs
Start	Bunnahabhain
	Grid ref: NR418734
Map	OS Explorer 353

This route makes for a challenging walk over some difficult terrain; however, the effort invested is very well rewarded. This is a truly spectacular walk around the remote north-eastern tip of Islay, which takes in some coastal scenery every bit as remarkable as that on the west coast of Jura. In fact, this section of Islay's coastline is a continuation of the rock platforms of Jura's west coast and is replete with the raised beaches, sea caves, rock stacks, basalt dikes and rock arches that are found there.

An alternative to walking out to Killinallan, is to return over the hill to Bunnahabhain from the coast south-west of Mala Bholsa. This variant route, which is included on the map and described after the Bunnhabhain – Killinallan route description, leaves the coast near the Stellaire Mor natural arch (NR372771). An advantage of taking this variant route is that walkers with their own transport can return to a car or bicycles left at Bunnahabhain. Using the postbus to get to and from Bunnahabhain to Keills is a possibility on schooldays, but this leaves just over eight hours to complete the walk, which is cutting it fine when breaks are factored in. Many postbus routes in the Highlands and Islands have been cut in recent years so check availability when planning your walk, call: 08457 740740. This variant route is slightly shorter than the Bunnahabhain – Killinallan route at approximately 20km (12 miles), although the rough terrain and extra height gain (250m) mean that it also takes seven to eight hours to complete. On a fine day, when conditions are clear, this variant also provides some excellent views across to Colonsay, Mull and beyond. However, when the ground is wet and visibility is poor this does not make for such a good option.

Just before the road bends and descends to the Bunnahabhain distillery buildings, there is a small parking area (NR418734). From here, follow the track heading west and after 100m turn north past some livestock pens and make for the gate in a deer fence. On the other side of the fence, follow the track that drops through a small deciduous copse, crossing the **Margadale River** on the footbridge before continuing north along the track. For the next 6km to **Rubh' a' Mhàil**, follow the ATV tracks where you can. In wet weather this section of the walk can be very boggy.

As you progress along the coast, there are fine views of two of Jura's Paps across the Sound of Islay – Beinn a' Chaolais and Beinn an Oir. A few kilometres beyond Bunnahabhain the Sgriob na Caillich can be seen descending west to the coast from the flank of Beinn an Oir. The 'old woman's slide' is a 3km-long belt of boulders deposited between convergent streams of the Devensian ice sheet that swept around and through the Paps from the east. It is regarded as the finest example of a fossil medial moraine in the British Isles.

Continuing north, the ATV tracks drop into the mouth of **Gleann Dubh**, cross the Allt an Achaidh then climb out again. As the tracks near Rhub' a' Mhàil, the slender white form of **Rhuvaal Lighthouse** comes into view (NR425802).

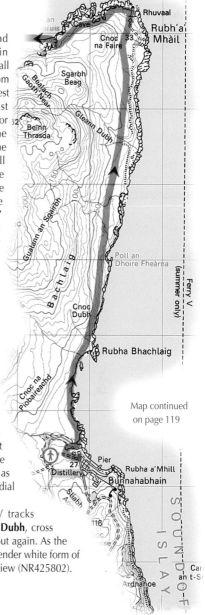

Map continued on page 119

THE LIGHTHOUSE STEVENSONS

Standing at nearly 36m (120ft), so as to cast its beam as far west as the Neva Rocks, the Rhuvaal Lighthouse was built between 1857 and 1859 to the design of David and Thomas Stevenson for the Northern Lighthouse Board.

The 'lighthouse Stevensons' were a Scottish engineering dynasty headed by Robert Stevenson, grandfather of the novelist and poet Robert Louis Stevenson. Of his family's engineering feats, he wrote: 'Whenever I smell salt water, I know I am not far from one of the works of my ancestors. The Bell Rock stands monument for my grandfather; the Skerry Vhor for my uncle Alan; and when the lights come out at sundown along the shores of Scotland, I am proud to think they burn more brightly for the genius of my father.'

Three generations of Stevensons built lighthouses, initially around Scotland's coast and then, as their reputation spread, they were engaged on projects as far afield as Japan and the Straits of Malacca.

East from Rubh' a' Mhàil there are views across to Loch Tarbert and Ruantallain; to the north lies Oronsay and Colonsay. Leaving the lighthouse behind, continue west, skirting above several long, steep-sided gullies that descend precipitously to the shore. At A' Bhriogais a fine basalt dike drops towards the sea like a massive rock groyne. Continue along the cliff-top, following the deer paths through the heather and you will soon arrive above the eastern end of the huge sandy beach at **Bàgh an Dà Dhoruis** ('bay of two doors'). Look out for a telegraph pole near the cliff edge and here you will find a path down to the beach (NR415788). This is a very fine beach even by Islay's high standards and its glory is crowned by a magnificent waterfall that descends from high above its eastern end.

Bàgh an Dà Dhoruis, west of Rhuvaal Lighthouse

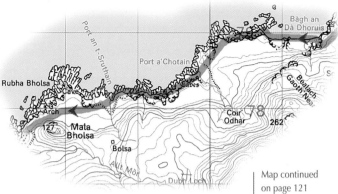

Map continued
on page 121

Once you've arrived on the beach it is possible to
walk along the shore for much of the remainder of this
route; however, there are a number of points where
a combination of tide and terrain make the shoreline
impassable. Indeed, several hundred metres beyond
Bàgh an Dà Dhoruis an impressively proportioned dike
blocks the way. In these instances it is no great effort to
take to the higher ground above the shore as little climbing is necessary. It is worth seeking every opportunity to
keep to the shore, however, as the undercliff route is full
of interest and beauty.

About 1km round the coast from Bàgh an Dà Dhoruis
you will arrive at **Port a' Chotain**, where you will find the
remains of an old stone 'sheiling', or shelter, and several
caves, including the impressively proportioned Uamh
Mhor or 'big cave' (NR398784). The entrance to the cave
is protected by a dry-stone wall and an enclosure. Some
distance beyond Port a' Chotain you will have to take to
higher ground for a while as the undercliff route is unnavigable around the point of **Rubha Bolsa**. Continue west
and skirt around the humpbacked flank of **Mala Bholsa** to
the south-west, staying above a large gully (NR377777).
If it is a fine day and you're feeling energetic, the summit
of Mala Bholsa (127m) makes a fine vantage point.

A short distance further on, descend into the amphitheatre at **Aonan na Mala**. Make for the rock arch on the
far side (NR373776), pass through it and emerge at the
foot of a gully. Climb the gully towards a low rock arch,
which frames a remarkable view into the next bay. Pass

119

through the arch and descend a gully to a burn, which can be tricky to cross when it is in spate. For the next few kilometres forge a route through a remarkable landscape of rock arches, waterfalls and small bays. Eventually, the undercliff route becomes largely impassable so leave the shore behind and you will soon find an ATV track winding a course along the higher ground some distance before it is marked on the OS map – where it is indicated as starting near the **Doodilmore River** (NR747343).

Follow the track across the river and continue for a further 1.5km to the **Gortantaoid River**. The river can be crossed before you reach the farmhouse at **Gortantaoid**. Follow the track through a livestock fence and continue on your way, heading south-west parallel with the eastern shore of Loch Gruinart sea loch, arriving at **Killinallan** after another 3km. The public road begins a 1500m further on and there is a small parking area there.

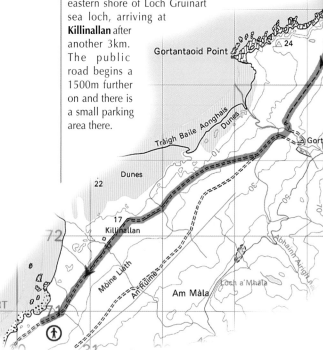

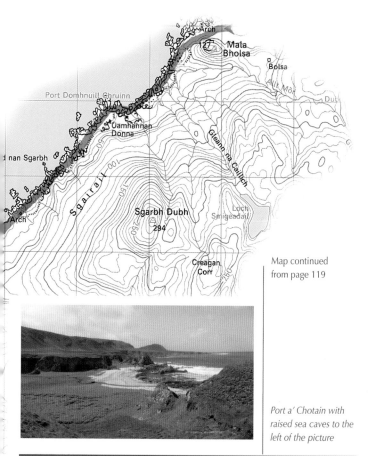

Arch

Mata
Bholsa

Bolsa

Allt Mòr

Port Domhnuill Ghruinn

Dui

Uamhannan
Donna

Gleann na Cailich

nan Sgarbh

Sgarbh

100

150

Sgarbh Dubh
294

Loch
Smigeadail

Arch

250

Creagan
Corr

250

Map continued
from page 119

*Port a' Chotain with
raised sea caves to the
left of the picture*

LOCH GRUINART

Loch Gruinart is an RSPB nature reserve with the wetlands, sandflats, dunes and saltmarshes of the area providing a habitat for resident and migratory species; most notably in October when large numbers of barnacle and white-fronted geese return from Greenland for the winter and spend a week or so on the flats of Loch Gruinart before dispersing to other areas of the island. Depending on when you visit, you may also see golden eagles, marsh harriers, hen harriers, peregrines, choughs, lapwings, ▶

curlews, snipes and many other species. There is an RSPB visitor centre at Aoradh at the head of the loch on the junction of the B8017 and the Ardnave road (NR276673).

Loch Gruinart was also the site of the last major clan battle to take place on Islay. In 1598, the Battle of Tràigh Ghruineard was fought between Sir Lachlan Mor MacLean, 14th Chief of Duart and his nephew Sir James MacDonald of Islay over possession of the Rinns of Islay, which Lachlan Mor claimed as a dowry given to his wife by her brother Angus MacDonald of Dunivaig and the Glens. As the battle reached its conclusion with Lachlan Mor slain, 30 MacLeans took flight and sought refuge in nearby Kilnave Chapel in the hope that the pursuing MacDonalds would respect sacred ground. They were given no quarter, however, and the roof of the chapel was torched; all but one of the MacLeans perished.

Variant return to Bunnahabhain from south-west of Mala Bholsa

For those choosing to walk this circular route variant, starting and finishing at Bunnahabhain, there are two reasons for leaving the coast near the Stellaire Mor natural arch (NR372771) for the return cross-country leg. Firstly, a fairly direct return route to Bunnahabhain can be navigated from here while taking to high ground to avoid some of the boggier terrain. Secondly, walking around the coast as far as Stellaire Mor gives walkers the opportunity to experience the best of this wonderful stretch of coastline – it would be a shame to walk this route and miss out on the extraordinary collection of natural features to be found along the kilometre of coast south-west of Mala Bholsa.

From the coastline by **Stellaire Mor** (NR372771), find an easy route on to the low cliff top. Head inland, south-east, using animal tracks where you can and climb gradually to the **Allt na Caillich** (NR375769). Cross the burn where the ground steepens and continue climbing south-east. Clearing the first steep rise you will see – if visibility allows – two hillocks just above 200m separated by a shallow col, about a kilometre ahead to the south-east. Climb towards this gap (NR386762) and turn to the east around the shoulder of the northerly of the two hillocks (219m). Cross a shallow and probably boggy gully and pass around a spur. From here, in good visibility, you will have views on to the western flank of **Sgarbh Breac** (364m). It is now a question of plotting a course just south of east, towards the pass (NR405759) between Sgarbh Breac and **Shùn Bheinn** to its south. Keeping south of **Loch Mhurchaidh** (NR397758) without losing too much height, try to pick as firm and dry a course across this boggy and tussocky stretch of ground as you can. When you arrive at the **Allt Bhachlaig** (NR405759),

cross the burn and pick up the ATV track running alongside it through the pass. If it is a clear day and you still have some energy, the summit of Sgarbh Breac offers some fine views of the Paps of Jura and much of Islay's hinterland. Otherwise, continue south-east along the track as it descends to the Sound of Islay and back to Bunnahabhain.

WALK 5

An Claddach–Beinn Bheigier circuit

Distance	Ballygrant to An Claddach 8km (5 miles); Beinn Bheigier circuit 16km (10 miles)
Time	Ballygrant to An Claddach 2hrs; Beinn Bheigier circuit 5–6hrs
Start	Ballygrant Grid ref: NR396663
Map	OS Explorer 353

At 491m, Beinn Bheigier, Islay's highest peak, is dwarfed by the Paps looming across the water on neighbouring Jura. However, a circular walk from An Claddach bothy on the Sound of Islay taking in Beinn Bheigier and several hills to its north, involves over 1035m (3400ft) – or a good Munro's worth – of ascent with the possibility of some fantastic views. The walk in to An Claddach from Ballygrant adds 8km (5 miles) and two hours to the route. You can avoid adding a further two hours to the day's walk – the return to Ballygrant – by spending a night or two at the bothy, using it as a base for walking and enjoying the sublime environment and plentiful wildlife. At high tide and/or in windy weather, certain sections of the route to or from An Claddach along the Sound of Islay can be difficult to negotiate.

Ballygrant to An Claddach bothy

Opposite the **Post Office** and shop in the centre of Ballygrant, take the minor road (NR396663) heading south-east for 500m. At a fork junction, keep left and follow a single-track road for a further 1.5km to **Lossit Farm**. Go through the farmyard, pass the house and outbuildings, then pass through a metal farm gate onto a track heading east. A sign reminds those taking to the hill during the stalking season (1 July until 15 February) to contact the estate office on 01496 840232 beforehand.

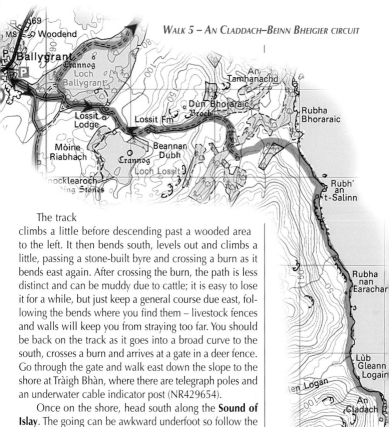

The track climbs a little before descending past a wooded area to the left. It then bends south, levels out and climbs a little, passing a stone-built byre and crossing a burn as it bends east again. After crossing the burn, the path is less distinct and can be muddy due to cattle; it is easy to lose it for a while, but just keep a general course due east, following the bends where you find them – livestock fences and walls will keep you from straying too far. You should be back on the track as it goes into a broad curve to the south, crosses a burn and arrives at a gate in a deer fence. Go through the gate and walk east down the slope to the shore at Tràigh Bhàn, where there are telegraph poles and an underwater cable indicator post (NR429654).

Once on the shore, head south along the **Sound of Islay**. The going can be awkward underfoot so follow the vague and often boggy path through the bracken fringing the beach. Continue along the shore for 3km to **An Claddach bothy**. This part of the route presents no real difficulties except at high tide or in rough weather when the narrowed stretches of shoreline a couple of hundred metres before and after crossing Abhainn Gleann Logain (NR436629) can be difficult to negotiate and may require a little scrambling to get around. In the summer months you should be able to cross the outflow of the Abhainn Gleann Logain at Lùb Gleann Logain; at other times, or when the river is in spate, there is a footbridge a couple of hundred metres upstream.

Map continued on page 128

On this stretch of coastline there are **splendid views** along the Sound of Islay and across the water to the southern end of Jura with, weather permitting, the Paps in all their glory. At the shoreline, keep an eye open for patrolling otters and curious seals. Great northern and red-throated divers hunt in the shallows, whooper swans cruise close to shore and oystercatchers dot around on the beach. Hen harriers and golden eagles often hunt around the Sound and adders are frequently found basking in the bracken above the shore.

The bothy occupies a splendid position just above the beach at An Claddach (NR439623), with views south-east along the Sound of Islay to McArthur's Head and beyond to the Isle of Gigha and the Kintyre peninsula. In clear conditions the mountains of Arran can be seen beyond Kintyre. ◄ Many happy hours can be spent watching the wildlife from the bench in front of the bothy. Adequate driftwood can usually be gleaned from nearby beaches and this is supplemented by peat and firewood brought by Donald James MacPhee, the Dunlossit Estate's head stalker, who is also a keen fell-runner.

An Claddach is a fine place to linger if you have the time.

An Claddach bothy on the Sound of Islay

AN CLADDACH BOTHY

An Claddach bothy was a derelict croft that was largely rebuilt by a Mountain Bothies Association work party during the summer of 1999. It is currently maintained by the MBA, by arrangement with the Dunlossit Estate. Restoration of the bothy was made possible by a bequest from Mr and Mrs Chadwick in memory of their son, Mike Chadwick, who died in Glencoe in 1994 aged 34.

Local tradition has it that the last occupant of the croft was one Baldy Claddach. He was renowned for being able to carry 10 stones of meal on his back over the hill from Ballygrant. Baldy was also reputed to be an illicit whisky distiller – an offence for which he was eventually transported to Canada, in around 1850. However, some suspect this was a pretext for clearing the land. Legend also maintains that Baldy's whisky is still out there, waiting to be found.

An Claddach–Beinn Bheigier circuit

Walk 100m or so north-west of the bothy and find your way up the flank of **Beinn Bhreac**, making for the ridge at the earliest opportunity. Once on the rocky spine of the ridge, the going underfoot is firmer and makes for easier walking. Continue to climb south-west up the ridge for the best part of 2km, following as it curves east onto the ridge of **Sgorr nam Faoileann**; the summit is reached after a further half-kilometre (NR434606). Although Sgorr nam Faoileann is of relatively modest height (429m), there are fine views from here in good weather. The length of the Sound of Islay and the curve of Jura's south-western coastline are visible to the north-east. To the north, Rhuvaal Lighthouse marks Islay's north-eastern extremity, with Colonsay visible beyond. To the north-west, the expanse of Loch Indaal is bordered by the Rinns of Islay, and Loch Gruinart may be visible beyond. Kintyre lies to the south-east across the North Channel.

Just over 1km south of the summit of Sgorr nam Faoileann as the crow flies is **Glas Bheinn**. Descend the southern flank of Sgorr nam Faoileann for around 180m, picking a route through the patches of scree and heather. Make for the dry-stone wall at the eastern side of the

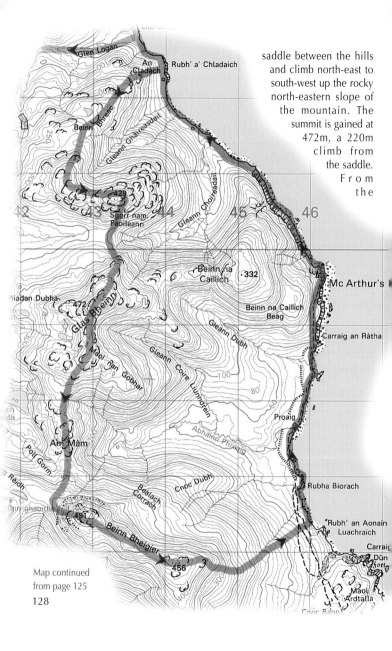

saddle between the hills and climb north-east to south-west up the rocky north-eastern slope of the mountain. The summit is gained at 472m, a 220m climb from the saddle. From the

Beinn Bheigier

top of Glas Bheinn there are views down to the bay at Proaig on the east coast and over to the humpbacked ridge of Beinn Bheigier lying 3km to the south.

Descend from the summit of Glas Bheinn via the gently gradiented south ridge, which delivers you to the col at 270m (NR425572) beneath the northern flank of **Beinn Bheigier** after 2km. From here, climb south to gain a second col on the west side of the mountain at around 350m (NR425567). From this second col, climb the remaining 140m east-south-east to the summit; a few vague paths help you on your way up through the heather and scree. There is an OS triangulation point on the summit with a small dry-stone wall shelter. Having enjoyed the views, head south-east along the summit ridge; there are several cairns at intervals along the way.

After 1km or so, you will arrive at the point where the ridge begins to drop away. Descend eastwards initially, then gradually bend a little north of east making for a point on the coast just north of **Rubh' an Aonain Luachraich** (NR460564). ▶ On arriving at the shore, however, life immediately becomes easier; head north, keeping to the vague path fringing the beach and after about 1km you will come to the outflow of the **Abhainn Phroaig**. Cross the river by means of two iron girders a short distance

The descent to the shore can be difficult going – boggy, tussocky and pathless.

129

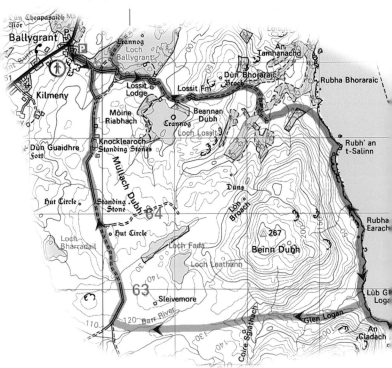

Map continued
on page 132

upstream. On the other side are the shepherd's cottage, sheepfold and outbuildings comprising the former settlement of Proaig. The cottage was re-roofed a few years ago and can be used as a bothy; however, cracks in the walls have led to birds nesting inside the building, making Proaig an inferior alternative shelter to An Claddach.

Continuing north along the shore from Proaig for 1km brings you to the foot of **Beinn na Caillich Beag** ('small hill of the old woman') on the far side of a lovely white sand beach. There is a vague path climbing north, which initially follows an exposed rock 'staircase'. The 'path' climbs to around 100m and continues north for several hundred metres before dropping towards the **McArthur's Head**

McArthur's Head Lighthouse on the Sound of Islay

Lighthouse, which, in common with Rhuvaal Lighthouse (1859), was built by David and Thomas Stevenson in 1861. From the lighthouse buildings, steps descend to the shore on the Sound of Islay. From here it is a further 3km back to An Claddach along the coast. ▶ Several hundred metres south of An Claddach an impressive section of basalt dike forms a natural sea wall.

It is worth looking out for otters on the way.

When returning from An Claddach there are several options. You can simply retrace your steps back along the coast, through **Lossit Farm** and along the road to **Ballygrant**. An alternative (marked in blue on the map) is to walk half a kilometre along the coast to the mouth of **Glen Logan**, then climb westwards up through the glen and across country making for the minor road north of **Storakaig**, roughly 4km from An Claddach. Once on the road, follow it north for a further 4km to Ballygrant. This route tends to be boggy.

If you're heading to **Port Askaig** for the ferry, there's the option (also marked in blue) of taking a track road through the woods and past the fishing lochs of the Dunlossit

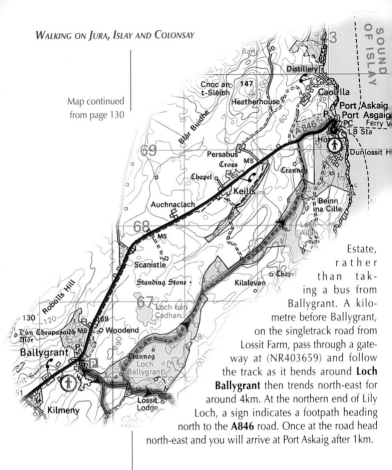

Map continued
from page 130

Estate,
rather
than tak-
ing a bus from
Ballygrant. A kilo-
metre before Ballygrant,
on the singletrack road from
Lossit Farm, pass through a gateway at (NR403659) and follow
the track as it bends around **Loch
Ballygrant** then trends north-east for
around 4km. At the northern end of Lily
Loch, a sign indicates a footpath heading
north to the **A846** road. Once at the road head
north-east and you will arrive at Port Askaig after 1km.

WALK 6
The Oa peninsula

Distance	Port Ellen to Kintra 25km (15½ miles)
Time	8–9hrs
Start	Junction of the B8016 and the Mull of Oa road next to the Port Ellen maltings
	Grid ref: NR362457
Map	OS Explorer 352

A walk around the entire Oa peninsula, which forms Islay's south-western extremity, makes for a very demanding day's walk. However, the effort invested is repaid with some wonderful coastal scenery and, in clear conditions, fine views of Kintyre, Arran, Rathlin Island, Antrim and the Rinns of Islay. There is also a good chance of spotting golden eagles, choughs and brown hares.

There are no paths for much of the route and the terrain is very demanding at times with boggy ground, heather and bracken cover, sizeable burns to negotiate and a number of livestock fences to cross. This is not a walk for very windy weather as the route traverses high clifftops leaving you very exposed; as well as being potentially hazardous, strong winds will make the walk extremely arduous.

If desired, the route can be halved by arranging a lift to or from the car park 1.5km (1mile) from the Mull of Oa itself and starting or finishing there (NR282423). The latter option is recommended, as the section from Port Ellen to the Mull of Oa has spectacular views. If walking the entire route to Kintra, you will need to arrange transport from there back to Port Ellen or walk the extra 5km (3 miles) on the road. If you are staying at Bowmore or beyond, another option is to head north along the sandy strand of Laggan Bay then cut across country to the bus stop at Islay Airport, which is a 4km walk from Kintra.

From the maltings head west along the minor road for 1km until you reach a small beech wood on the seaward

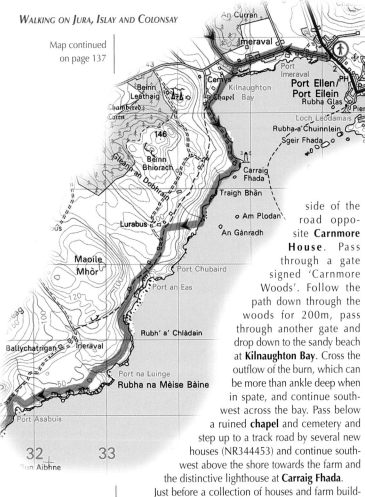

Map continued
on page 137

side of the road opposite **Carnmore House**. Pass through a gate signed 'Carnmore Woods'. Follow the path down through the woods for 200m, pass through another gate and drop down to the sandy beach at **Kilnaughton Bay**. Cross the outflow of the burn, which can be more than ankle deep when in spate, and continue southwest across the bay. Pass below a ruined **chapel** and cemetery and step up to a track road by several new houses (NR344453) and continue southwest above the shore towards the farm and the distinctive lighthouse at **Carraig Fhada**.

Just before a collection of houses and farm buildings, a signpost indicates a path to the 'Singing Sands'; follow this up a slight rise before passing through a gate and continuing along the path indicated by a second signpost. Pass through another gate after 200m and descend to the sandy beach at Tràigh Bhàn, known as the Singing Sands because of the sound made by the wind-blown sand. ◄

From here on you are almost certain to encounter tribes of wild goats.

Continue along the beach, then through rocky terrain following goat tracks to another smaller bay.

From Alt an t-Seilich (NR343436), find a route up from the shore – through bracken in the summer months – and make your way south-west up towards the obvious house on the skyline. You may have to cross a livestock fence en route before emerging onto a track road just to the rear of the house. Follow the track for 20m to a junction then turn left and head south-west through a gate next to some stone ruins. The path descends a little, passing more ruins before arriving at a burn, which runs out to a waterfall (NR336429). Cross the burn and then cross the adjacent livestock fence to the clifftop side. The path is vague here, but runs close to the fence for 200m before crossing a basic stile.

Continue along the vague path, which mostly follows the course of the fence. ▶

There are splendid views of the coastline with its beaches, coves, cliffs and rocky shoreline, but keep well away from the cliff edge.

Arriving above **Port na Luinge**, a massive wall-like basalt dike drops down to the shore; keep to the tracks that descend south-west to a burn above the far side of the bay. Cross the burn opposite an obvious stile crossing a livestock fence (NR327415). Head south up a slight incline and after 200m cross to the clifftop side of the fence. Continue along the clifftops for half a kilometre or so before crossing a burn that drops into a gully full of farm detritus. There are livestock fences to cross on either side of the gully (NR320412). Stay inside the fence for a few hundred metres, then recross to the clifftop side of the fence above the east side of **Port Asabuis**. Make your way around to a gate in a livestock fence (NR316410) above the far side of Port Asabuis by following a vague path up to a farm track heading south-west. Follow the farm track for 40m or so before heading south to the gate.

Pass through the gate and continue along the clifftop for half a kilometre before dropping in to a deep gully, crossing a burn and climbing out again. Cross a fence, continue south-east and pass through a gate (NR310403).

In summer, the bracken cover along this stretch can be head-high in places.

Climbing towards Beinn Mhor

A distinct path then climbs steeply west to higher ground above the rising cliffs, levelling out at about 100m. Try to follow goat tracks through the close-covering heather, which can make the going difficult. After a few hundred metres,

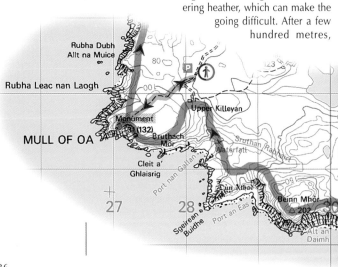

the ground climbs again to the trig point atop the high point of **Beinn Mhor** at 202m (NR295405). There are dramatic views from here in clear conditions; across the sea to the coasts of Kintyre and Antrim; inland to Islay's hinterland; and westwards across the high cliffs to the Mull of Oa and the sentinel-like American Monument, with the Rinns of Islay beyond.

Descend north-west from Beinn Mhor, staying above the clifftop with fine views down to **Port an Eas** and the site of the Bronze Age fortification of Dùn Athad upon its anvil-like, quartzite promontory. After losing a little height, follow the vague path that contours around to the slope descending to the Bealach nan Crann (NR286410) rather than dropping too precipitously to the clifftop. ▶ If you're finishing your walk at the Mull of Oa car park for example – otherwise cross the bealach and skirt above **Port nan Gallan** until you arrive at the small gully through which the **Sruthan Rabhairt** flows (NR285414).

Cross the burn and climb out of the gully onto a track, which is part of a dedicated footpath leading to the Mull of Oa. The track is often very muddy, but it is extensively waymarked. Follow it north-west towards **Upper Killeyan**, crossing a fence by a stile before crossing a burn by means of duckboards. Follow the waymarkers as they climb towards the farm then pass through a gate, heading south-west on level ground before passing through a second gate. Continue along the clifftops for a further 750m to arrive at the American Monument on the **Mull of Oa**.

Port an Eas is certainly worth exploring if you have the time.

The Mull of Oa and the American Monument

THE AMERICAN MONUMENT

The imposing monument, erected in 1920, resembles a lighthouse and it commemorates nearly 700 American soldiers who were lost in two separate disasters in 1918. In February of that year, the *SS Tuscania*, a troopship transporting more than 2000 soldiers from the US, was torpedoed 7 miles off the Mull of Oa by a German submarine. Despite rescue attempts, 266 soldiers and sailors either drowned or died when their lifeboats were dashed against the cliffs of the Oa. In October 1918 two troopships, *HMS Otranto* and *HMS Kashmir*, collided in a heavy storm off the coast and the *Otranto* sank in Machir Bay with the loss of 431 lives. The dead were buried in Kilchoman cemetery overlooking Machir Bay, but the Americans were exhumed in 1920 to be repatriated or reinterred in the American military cemetery at Brookwood, Surrey. There are 73 British and Commonwealth sailors and marines from the *Otranto* buried at Kilchoman military cemetery, 43 of whom are unidentified.

If you are finishing your walk at the Mull of Oa car park, follow the waymarkers heading inland to the north-east, away from the cliffs. There are stiles and gates through livestock fences and duckboards over boggy ground; the car park is reached after 1.5km.

If you are continuing to Kintra, follow the way-marked path inland for a few hundred metres before turning north along the coast again. As you leave the monument behind, the remaining 10km to Kintra may appear to be a gentle stroll across gradually diminishing clifftops. This is not the case. There are several steep-sided valleys and sizeable burns to negotiate as well as boggy ground, heather and bracken cover and a number of livestock fences to cross. ▶

This is an impressive stretch of coastline with many interesting natural and man-made features, and there are fine views west across Loch Indaal to the Rinns of Islay.

The clifftop route is easy enough at first, especially if you follow the vague paths through the heather. The first obstacle is the burn running through the **An Gleann** gully (NR275431), south-west of the small settlement of Lower Killeyan. This is easy enough to cross; however, half a kilometre or so further on you will arrive at Abhainn Ghil, which is too wide to jump and has to be forded. After crossing the burn, skirt around the hillside above the bay at Alt a' Ghamhna then continue on, keeping to the landward side of a pair of distinctive hillocks (NR274439). Cross a small burn and a fence then continue on your way along the clifftops through close heather cover and sporadic thickets of bracken, gaining or losing a little height and crossing the occasional fence or burn. There is a significant drop into and climb out of **Lower Glen Astle**, but the Abhainn Alt Astail running through it is easy to cross.

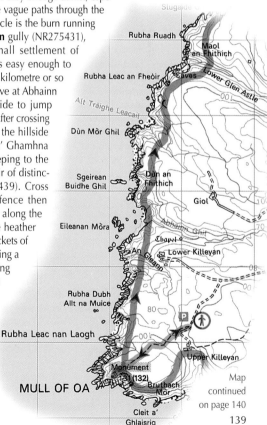

Map continued on page 140

Having gained the high ground north of Lower Glen Astle, contour above the clifftops by the easiest route available. After 1.5km the terrain slopes down towards lower ground around Poll nan Gamhna. Cross the Sruthan Poll nan Gamhna (NR296476) and head towards the sea, recrossing the burn before it drops into a deepening gully. Follow the edge of the gully and cross a rock arch in the cliff; from here there is a spectacular view of the Soldier's Rock stack and the waterfall carrying the Sruthan Poll nan Gamhna to the sea. Retrace your steps until you can continue along the coast, following goat tracks and keeping well above the rocky shore. After a further 1.5km you will come to a dense area of small birch trees. The ground is boggy and the woods are tricky to cross. On exiting the woods you will find a trodden path that leads around a couple of small bays before

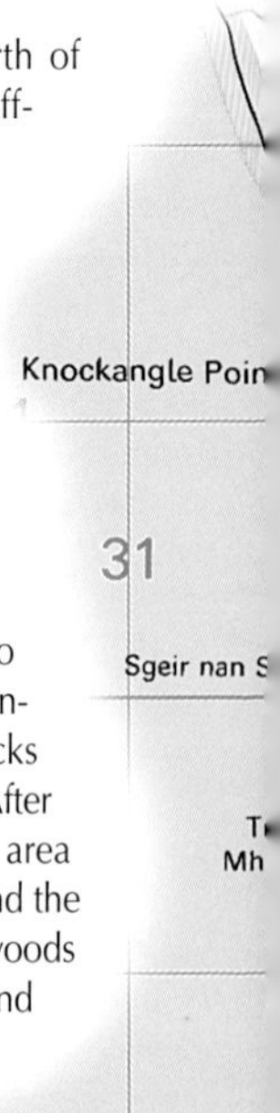

Knockangle Poin

31

Sgeir nan S

T
Mh

Map continued
from page 139

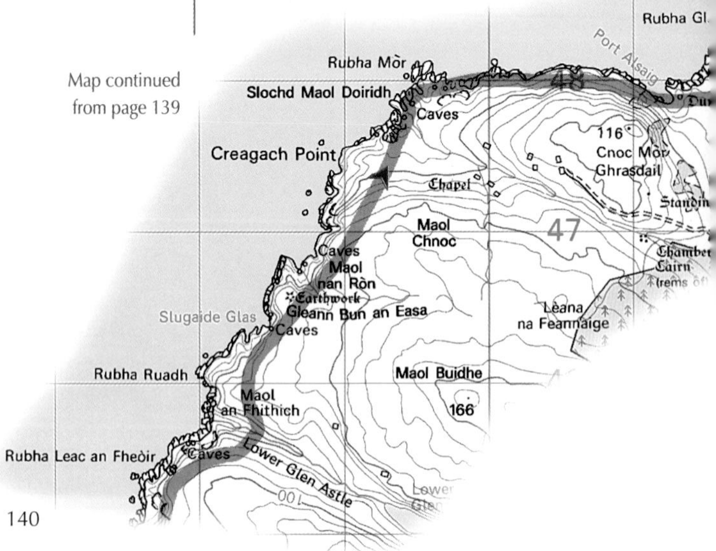

Rubha Mòr
Slochd Maol Doiridh
Caves
Creagach Point
Chapel
Maol
Chnoc
Caves
Maol
nan Ròn
Earthwork
Slugaide Glas
Gleann Bun an Easa
Caves
Rubha Ruadh
Maol
an Fhithich
Maol Buidhe
166
Rubha Leac an Fheòir
Caves
Lower Glen Astle
Lower

Rubha Gl

Port Alsaig

48
Dun

116
Cnoc Mòr
Ghrasdail

Standin

47
Chamber
Cairn
trems

Leana
na Feannaige

100

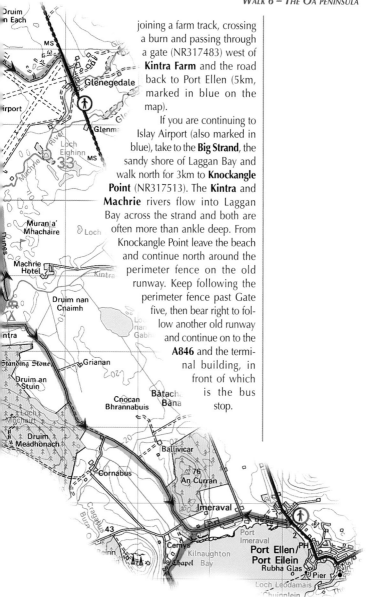

joining a farm track, crossing a burn and passing through a gate (NR317483) west of **Kintra Farm** and the road back to Port Ellen (5km, marked in blue on the map).

If you are continuing to Islay Airport (also marked in blue), take to the **Big Strand**, the sandy shore of Laggan Bay and walk north for 3km to **Knockangle Point** (NR317513). The **Kintra** and **Machrie** rivers flow into Laggan Bay across the strand and both are often more than ankle deep. From Knockangle Point leave the beach and continue north around the perimeter fence on the old runway. Keep following the perimeter fence past Gate five, then bear right to follow another old runway and continue on to the **A846** and the terminal building, in front of which is the bus stop.

WALK 7
Sanaigmore to Kilchiaran

Distance	17km (11 miles)
Time	5hrs
Start	Small parking area at the end of the B8018 near Sanaigmore Farm Grid ref: NR236707
Map	OS Explorer 353

This walk along Islay's Atlantic coast takes in some of the island's finest bays as well as dramatic sea cliffs and rocky shores. The walk suits all seasons and weathers; on a sunny day the turquoise waters and white sands sparkle with reflected light; in windy conditions, huge waves crash against the shore demonstrating the awesome power of the sea.

The terrain is generally less challenging than on most of the previous walks described. There are more tracks and paths to follow and less bracken and heather cover to negotiate. There are a number of livestock fences to be crossed, however. For the fit and determined, the route can be extended by starting at Ardnave Point, north-east of Sanaigmore, adding a tough 10km (6 miles) and 3–4hrs to the walk (see Walk 8).

There are no buses to Sanaigmore, so you will need to arrange your own transport. The same applies at Kilchiaran, although the 5km (3 miles) walk from there to Port Charlotte on the east coast of the Rinns of Islay is manageable at the end of this walk.

Next to the parking area stands the **Exmouth memorial**. This cairn-like monument commemorates the 241 Irish emigrants who perished when the *Exmouth Castle*, en route from Londonderry to Quebec, was wrecked upon the rocks at Geodha Ghille Mhòire, 2km to the west, during violent storms in April 1847. The only survivors were three of the ship's crew.

Follow the path leading north from the memorial to a farm gate. Pass through and head down to the bay. Highland cows graze in the fields here; they're usually docile but keep your distance and avoid getting between adults and their calves. Take some time to appreciate this beautiful bay before continuing north-west along the coast. There is a vague path in places, but stay close to the shore initially to avoid some very boggy ground. After a few hundred metres the ground rises a little and a more definite ATV track steers a course above the beautiful, steep-sided little bay of Port Ghille Greamhair – a wonderful place for a swim in calm conditions.

Continue on the ATV track as it passes inside and then follows the course of a dry-stone wall. The ground can be very boggy and a few old duckboards help out here and there. The terrain rises towards the rugged and hilly headland, which drops away to high cliffs and a rocky coastline on the seaward side. It's worth exploring this dramatic headland before continuing along the track as it turns south-west (NR228714) and skirts beneath the higher ground. The track descends gradually in to **Gleann Tuath**, bounded on the south-east by

Map continued on page 145

the rock-faced flank of Cnoc an Tigh, and arrives above the shore overlooking the beach of **Tràigh Bhàn** at the head of a broad inlet. Here there is a monument to those who perished in the 'Exmouth Sea Tragedy'; 108 bodies were washed ashore here and are buried beneath the dunes.

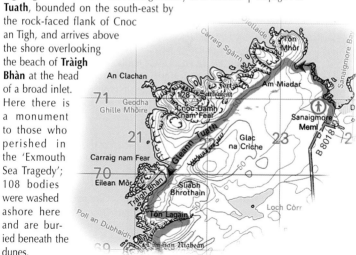

Dùn Bheolain – the 'Opera House Rocks'

Dùn Bheolain is known locally as the Opera House Rocks because of its striking resemblance to Sydney's famous concert hall.

From the memorial, cross a small burn and head south up a steep slope to pass through a gate (NR215699). Follow sheep tracks that contour around the coast for half a kilometre to gain fantastic views of a very distinctive promontory named for the hill fort that once sat atop it, of which only traces remain. ◀

From a distance it looks as if there might be a way around the coast at the neck of the Dùn Bheolain promontory, but this isn't the case. Instead, head east up a small glen until you find a way up onto the hill that forms the glen's southern flank (NR216695). Follow tracks through the heather to the dry-stone wall at the south-western edge of the hill for another great view of Dùn Bheolain. Cross the wall, which is also topped by a wire fence, and descend by a grassy slope to the foot of the cliff forming the hill's south-eastern flank.

Make for a wooden gate in a dry-stone wall to the south and pass through it. For the next 1km the route crosses a series of gates and stiles with the odd stretch of path through low-lying terrain. On reaching **Tràigh Flèisgein Bheag**, cross the beach and pick up an ATV track on the far side. Follow this until it turns inland. Continue above the shore until you find a viable way down to the sands of **Saligo Bay**; the northern reaches are cut off from the rest of the bay at high tide.

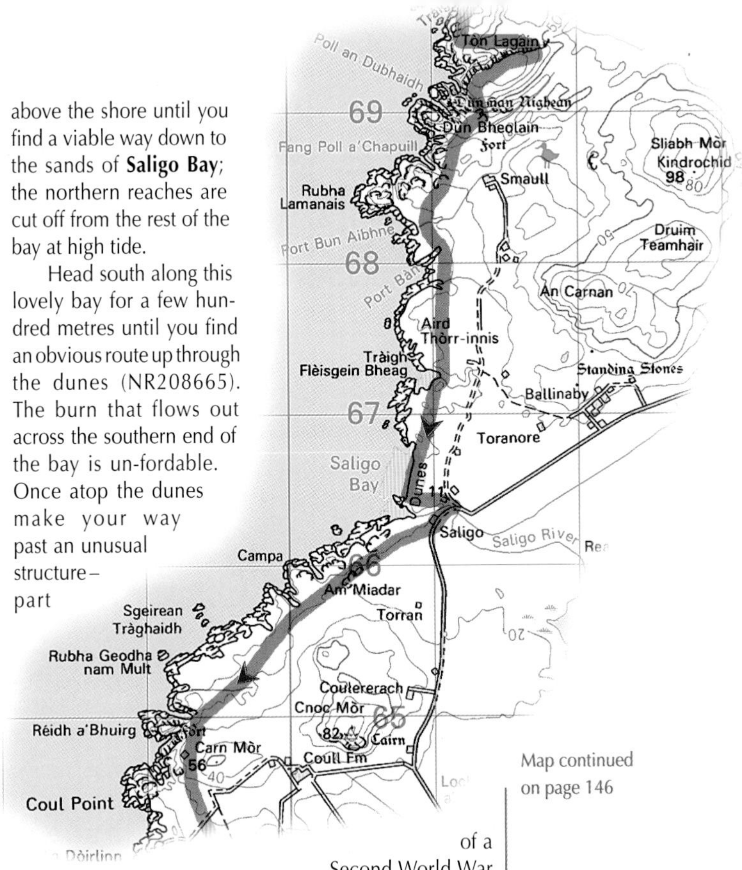

Head south along this lovely bay for a few hundred metres until you find an obvious route up through the dunes (NR208665). The burn that flows out across the southern end of the bay is un-fordable. Once atop the dunes make your way past an unusual structure – part of a Second World War radar station that includes several nearby bunkers – and make for the gate next to the bridge (NR212664), turning right onto the road. After passing a row of cottages on your right go through a wooden gate with a sign reading 'To the Arches'. A vague path crosses boggy ground and passes through a gap in a dry-stone wall. The path soon becomes more distinct and after 1km the advertised natural arches are reached. A few hundred metres beyond the arches, pass through a gate in a dry-stone wall.

Continue on your way and after half a kilometre gain a little height as you make for a derelict observation post

Map continued on page 146

145

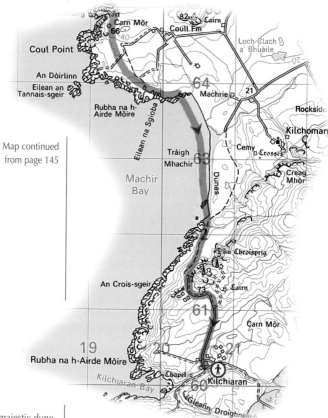

Map continued
from page 145

The majestic dune-backed expanse of white sand that is Machir Bay stretches for nearly 2km and is an absolute joy to walk along with the Atlantic rolling or crashing ashore beside you.

on the western flank of **Carn Mòr**. Descend to the south crossing one livestock fence and making for a gate in another fence running along the coast a few hundred metres further on. However, keep to the inside and follow it to a junction of fences across a burn a few hundred metres further on (NR195642). Cross here to the outside of the fence and continue along the sporadically boggy coast for a further 1km, crossing two more fences, to arrive at **Machir Bay**. ◄

Machir Bay

Walk to the southern end of the bay and make for the track that climbs directly from the beach then passes through a gate and continues to climb beneath the radar station perched atop Creag a' Chaorainn and Creag Goirtean na Feannaige. The metalled track passes through a second gate, then winds up and over the Bealach na Caillich ('old woman's pass') before dropping down to the road (NR206603) near **Kilchiaran Farm** 1km to the south. The nearby ruins of 14th-century Kilchiaran Chapel, with its Mediaeval tombstones and baptismal font are well worth a visit.

WALK 8
Ardnave to Sanaigmore

Distance	10km (6 miles)
Time	4hrs
Start	Parking area by Ardnave Loch
	Grid ref: NR287728
Map	OS Explorer 353

It is possible to extend the Sanaigmore to Kilchiaran route (Walk 7) by starting at Ardnave, some 10km (6 miles) to the north-east of Sanaigmore. The terrain is challenging: there are no paths and densely growing heather makes the going tough; the ground is also boggy in places and several livestock fences need to be crossed. However, this stretch of coastline has an understated beauty and you are unlikely to see anyone else once you are a couple of kilometres south-west of Ardnave Point. Alternatively, an enjoyable half-day can be spent walking around the point itself, starting and finishing at the parking area by Ardnave Loch.

If the tide isn't high and you're not continuing on to Sanaigmore, the shore makes for a pleasant route to Ardnave Point.

From the parking area, head north-east along the track signposted for 'Tayvullin and the Beach'. After 100m or so, the track bends to the east and 100m further on turns sharply north-east. Were you to continue to the east, you would pass through the dunes to arrive on the sandy shore of **Loch Gruinart**. ◄ Otherwise, continue on the main route above the dunes for 1.5km until you come to signpost indicating 'Viewpoint Nave Island Otters and Seals'. Follow the sign north-west to arrive on the shore at Tràigh nam Fuaran (NR287746), south-west of Ardnave Point, with a fine view of Nave Island. Seals can be seen on the offshore skerries and gannets often dive-bomb for fish in this area.

Head south-west along the sandy shore, before negotiating a short rocky stretch, which can be slippery when wet, then cross a fence to arrive on the fine, dune-backed beach at **Tràigh Nòstaig**. Carry on along the shore to Port na Muic at the far end of Tràigh Nòstaig, where you will find a curious structure – apparently a disused lobster farm. Follow the obvious track up a slight incline towards a gate

(NR277736) and pass through it, continuing south-west. However, if you are returning to Ardnave Loch, follow the track that initially heads north-east then bends around to the south-east and passes through Ardnave Farm before arriving at the loch once more. Otherwise, skirt around the small bay, fringed with an area of raised pebble beach to the south and west and continue, gaining a little height, through coastal moorland that can be rather boggy.

For the next 1km or so, forge a route a couple of hundred metres back from the shore until you arrive at the broad gully leading down to the flotsam and jetsam scattered pebble beach at Port Bhreac Achaidh. Cross the gully at its top end passing over a basic stile in a livestock fence (NR266727). Work your way around the coast, staying

Map continued on page 148

149

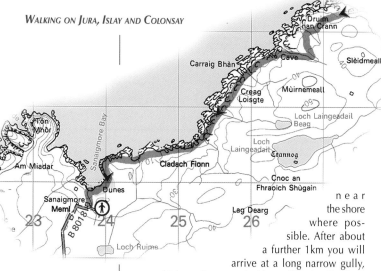

near the shore where possible. After about a further 1km you will arrive at a long narrow gully, which can be crossed without difficulty. Continue on your way until you reach a dry-stone wall, which you should cross before making for the rock-studded sandy beach a short distance to the south-west. Find a route along the sandy shore between the rocks until the tide or the end of the beach send you back to higher ground. Cross a raised pebble beach and pick up an ATV track by **Cladach Fionn** (NR247714), which you can follow through a couple of fences and across a ford until it bends sharply to the south. Leave the track here and continue above the shore until you reach the eastern end of **Sanaigmore** a couple of hundred metres further on.

Coastline north-east of Sanaigmore

150

COLONSAY

Above Pig's Paradise on Colonsay's west coast (Walk 10)

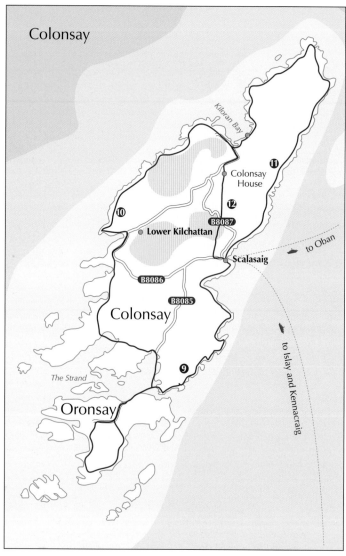

INTRODUCTION

Kiloran Bay from Carnan Eoin (Walk 10)

At a combined length of 15km (9½ miles) and 5km (3 miles) across the widest point, Colonsay and its tide-separated sister island of Oronsay are small enough to circumnavigate in two days. However, the great natural beauty and peaceful atmosphere of the islands will persuade most walkers to take a little more time exploring.

The word remote is often applied to Colonsay and Oronsay; they lie 15km west of Jura, some 40km west of the Argyll mainland, 9km north of Islay and 25km south of Mull. Westwards is the Atlantic, with only Dubh Artach Lighthouse standing between Colonsay and Canada. However, the wild and rugged terrain

one might expect in such an exposed situation forms only part of the picture. Though small, these islands possess great scenic variety; the moorland, hills and rocky outcrops of the interior overlook some remarkably verdant terrain, including tracts of indigenous woodland and exotic plantation, and a coastline garlanded with magnificent sandy bays, small coves, raised beaches, towering cliffs and outlying skerries.

The islands' compact scale and modest hills tend not to detain clouds on their way to the hills of Jura, Islay and Kintyre, affording summer sunshine hours on a par with Tiree – the sunniest place in Scotland. The annual rainfall is half that of mainland Argyll and the temperature rarely drops below two or three degrees in winter. The mild climate provides suitable conditions for a wide range of plants, flowers and trees that flourish, most notably in the exotic woodland and gardens of Colonsay House at Kiloran.

Colonsay has a population of scarcely more than 100 and the main settlements are the east coast port of Scalasaig, which has the island's only general store, post office and hotel, Lower Kilchattan (the 'c' is silent) to the west and Kiloran to the north-west. Much of the island's employment centres around management of the Colonsay Estate, tourism, agriculture and a number of small businesses including the Colonsay Brewery at Scalasaig. Many islanders are multi-taskers who fulfil a number of roles in the community, including staffing the lifeboat and fire services as well as working at the ferry port or bookshop, or driving the school bus. The community has had some difficulty hanging on to its younger population in recent years and in a move to redress population decline a grant-aided initiative – the Colonsay Croft Project – has been established to encourage resourceful individuals, couples or families to build new crofts and set up small businesses.

Oronsay, or Oransay as most locals seem to prefer, is only accessible for a maximum of three hours either side of low-tide (see below) across a 1km-wide sand flat known as The Strand.

The island is largely low-lying with Beinn Oronsay rising to 93m to the north-west. The only habitation is on Oronsay Farm, which sits at the foot of Beinn Oronsay next to the ruins of the 14th-century Augustinian priory. The 2001 census recorded Oronsay as having a population of just five people living and working at Oronsay Farm. The entire island is an RSPB Nature Reserve, designated Site of Special Scientific Interest (SSSI) and Special Protection Area (SPA) for its corncrake and chough populations. Oronsay is farmed by the RSPB with a mixed livestock (cattle and sheep) and arable crops regime.

HISTORY

The earliest settlers arrived on Colonsay and Oronsay from the mainland of Argyll around 7000BC. In recent years the islands' Mesolithic period has been extensively studied with excavations undertaken at several sites on Oronsay and at Staosnaig on Colonsay. The artefacts and animal remains recovered from these sites have provided much information about the early settlers' way of life and radiocarbon dating has established a timescale for the period of early settlement.

Of particular note are the six Mesolithic 'shell-mounds' found on Oronsay, which are up to 30m in diameter and 3.5m high and are largely composed of midden material – primarily limpet shells – and layers of blown sand. One such mound, Caisteal nan Gillean, was excavated between 1879 and 1882 by J Symington Grieve, who recovered bone and stone tools dating from the Mesolithic period.

More recently, radiocarbon dating of materials recovered from excavations at six sites on Oronsay suggests a relatively brief though intense period of exploitation of the island's natural resources by the Mesolithic settlers, around the middle of the fifth millennium BC. Innovation in excavation techniques and more sophisticated analysis may also determine whether the various tools discovered in different environments belong to distinct groups or to one group exploiting a diverse range of natural resources according to seasonal availability.

In common with Jura, there are no recorded traces of Neolithic settlement on Colonsay and Oronsay, although settlement sites and burial cairns have been found on Islay and Mull. However, stone axes found at Balnahard and flint arrowheads recovered on Oronsay are evidence of inhabitation during the period (4000–2000BC). By the early fourth millennium BC, in what is present-day Argyll, the itinerant hunter-gatherers were settling into permanent agriculture-based communities employing new livestock-rearing and crop-growing skills imported from mainland Europe.

Farms and fortifications

Archaeological sites dating from the Bronze Age (c2500–600BC) on Colonsay and Oronsay include hut circles, field systems, burial cairns, cists and standing stones such as 'Fingal's Limpet Hammers' at Lower Kilchattan. Although archaeological investigation of Bronze Age sites has been limited, evidence points to the existence of small farming communities at sites such as Lower Kilchattan and Uragaig during the earlier part of the second millennium BC.

Along with the other Inner Hebridean islands and the Kintyre peninsula, Colonsay and Oronsay were colonised by the Scotti of Dál Riata from the north of Ireland around the fifth century. The colonisers brought Iron Age (c600BC–AD400) technologies with them and their legacy is evident in the Iron Age fortifications dotted around the islands. There are eight Iron Age forts on Colonsay and Oronsay, including Dun Cholla, Dun Domhnuill, Dun Eibhinn, Dun Gallain and Dun Meadhonach, as well as 13 duns, which are smaller fortifications. Colonsay has a relatively high number of duns compared with the rest of Argyll, which may reflect the island's fertility; their presence is associated with land under cultivation.

Early Christian missionaries followed in the wake of the Dalriadans. In AD563 St Columba and his followers arrived in the Inner Hebrides from Ireland. Columba is said to have first landed on Oronsay, but on discovering that his beloved Ireland was still visible from the summit of Beinn Oronsay he continued his voyage, eventually landing at Iona where he founded a monastery.

Viking presence

At the end of the eighth century the Vikings first appeared in the seas around the Inner Hebrides, raiding and plundering monasteries, including Iona. The Norse presence on Colonsay and Oronsay from the early ninth century is evidenced by several Viking burial sites including a boat burial at Lagg na Birlinn ('hollow of the boat') in the dunes behind Kiloran Bay. The similar numbers of men and women among the burials suggests the presence of permanent settlers rather than raiders. No structures attributable to Norse settlers have been identified on Colonsay and Oronsay, though there is evidence that forts and duns were reoccupied. Norse place names are found on both islands, and Colonsay and Oronsay are known to have been part of the Norse Kingdom of Man and the Isles until the early 13th century.

The Norse sphere of influence in the Inner Hebrides was undermined when Somerled divided the Norse Kingdom of Man and the Isles by defeating Godred's forces in a sea battle off the west coast of Islay in 1156. Somerled's descendants, named Clan Donald and known as the Lords of the Isles, subsequently took control of the entire west coast and parts of northern Scotland, which they ruled from their seat of power at Finlaggan on Islay.

Rebellion

During the Middle Ages the islands lay within the MacDonald Lordship of the Isles, with Oronsay and part of south Colonsay granted to Oronsay Priory. Colonsay was held through the agency of the MacDuffies or MacFies who retained the island on lease from the Scottish Crown following the forfeiture of the MacDonald's lands in 1493. In 1614–15, Sir James MacDonald of Islay unsuccessfully attempted to regain the MacDonald

Looking south-west from Beinn Oronsay with the priory ruins and Oronsay Farm below and Islay on the horizon (Walk 9)

inheritance by force and Malcolm MacFie of Colonsay who was instrumental in the rebellion was captured and handed over to the Earl of Argyll. He returned to Colonsay upon his release from custody and was subsequently murdered in 1623 by Coll Kittoch MacDonald (Col Ciotach Mac Domhnaill), who then became Laird of Colonsay and held the island peacefully for some years.

Later in the 17th century, Colonsay and Oronsay were incorporated into the expanding earldom of Argyll, but in 1701 the 10th Earl of Argyll sold the islands to Malcolm McNeill of Crear in Knapdale. During the 19th century, the inhabitants escaped the worst of the clearances due to the enlightened agricultural policies of laird John McNeil. The estate stayed in the McNeil family until the death of Sir John Carstairs McNeill in 1904, when it was purchased by the 1st Lord Strathcona. It remains in the hands of the Strathcona family today.

GEOLOGY

Among the most fertile islands of the Hebrides, Colonsay and Oronsay are largely formed of sedimentary rocks of Lower Torridonian age – between 1200 and 800 million years old – comprising layers of limestone, phyllites, mudstones, flags, grits and conglomerates. Kiloran flags, the strata underlying the limestone, form much of the islands' hilly interior. Igneous intrusive rocks outcrop at Scalasaig and to the north there are numerous lamprophyre dikes of widely different ages, while tertiary basalt dikes are encountered in the south. Colonsay and Oronsay lie at the south-west end of the Great Glen Fault, with the main line running to the east of the islands.

During the glacial period the ice sheet flowed south-westwards over the islands from the centre of the ice cap in the area of Rannoch Moor. The passage of the ice sheet ground and smoothed the rock with the characteristic east-west striations caused by

Raised beaches south of Lower Kilchattan

glacier-borne stones. When the glaciers retreated, these 'erratic' boulders, including specimens of Glen Fyne granite, were left behind. Other phenomena resulting from the withdrawal of the ice sheet are the raised beaches of the west coast, such as those south of Lower Kilchattan, the caves and rock arches on the west coast around Uragaig and the pre-glacial sea cliffs, most notably between Scalasaig and Machrins, at Uragaig and south of Balnahard. The weight of the ice cap depressed the landmass and when it melted the sea level rose and the land gradually rebounded, continuing long after the sea level reached its maximum, resulting in the exposure of a formerly submarine coastline.

Raised wave-cut platforms and raised beaches have formed the basis of well-drained land that has been cultivated since the first settlement of the islands. The most fertile areas have soils that originated in raised beach deposits laid down when parts of the island were under the sea. This includes the arable land around Garvard, Ardskenish, Machrins, Lower Kilchattan, Kiloran, Balnahard and Oronsay. Much of Colonsay's hilly interior and parts of the east coast are cloaked in a layer of peat on which bracken, heather, myrtle, sedges and mosses thrive. The influence of the Atlantic on much of the coastline has led to the development of significant areas of fertile, low-lying sand dune pasture, or 'machair', formed when sand with a high seashell content is blown inland, neutralising the acidity of peat soils and propagating fertile grassland. In late spring and summer, the machair is festooned with a multicoloured riot of wild flowers. The areas around Kiloran and Balnahard bays and much of Oronsay are fine examples of machair pasture.

WILDLIFE

In a relatively small area, Colonsay and Oronsay possess a wide variety of natural habitats including moorland, peat bogs, fresh water lochs, meadow and pasture land, arable farmland, ancient forest and cultivated woodland, dunes, machair, raised shingle beaches, sandy beaches, tidal flats, sea cliffs and rocky shoreline, as well as offshore islands and reefs.

The obvious major difference from Islay and Jura in particular is the absence of deer. Jura's vast wild interior is the perfect habitat for its large population of red deer; Colonsay's only 'wilderness' is confined to a few square kilometres in its north-east corner. This area is the domain of the island's wild goat population, which – in common with their cousins on Jura and Islay – are said to be descended from animals that arrived on the island from ships of the Spanish Armada wrecked nearby.

In common with other Scottish islands, there are many terrestrial mammals present on the mainland that are absent from Colonsay and Oronsay. Those present include the brown hare, rabbit, pygmy shrew,

Wild goats on Colonsay's wild east coast

wood mouse, brown rat and pipist-relle bat. The European or Eurasian otter is well established with territories all around the islands; the chances of seeing an otter while walking around the coast are quite good.

Marine mammals include the common and grey seal; there are robust colonies on offshore islands around Oronsay and the south-west coast of Colonsay. Seals can also be seen basking along rocky stretches of coastline or scanning the shore from many of the bays and coves around the islands. The high cliffs around Pigs Paradise and Meall Lamalum on Colonsay's west coast provide a van-tage point for observing seals in their element. Common dolphins, basking sharks and minke whales are occa-sionally seen off the coast of Colonsay

and Oronsay; other varieties of dol-phin, porpoise and whale are infre-quent. Two reptiles are also found on the islands, the slow worm and com-mon lizard. There are no snakes.

Almost 200 species of bird have been recorded on Colonsay and Oronsay in recent years and the islands are particularly noted for their populations of chough and corncrake. The corncrake, whose rasping call presages the onset of spring, is one of Britain's rarest birds and has become something of an island mascot. Corncrakes are more often heard than seen. Oronsay is a good place to hear them and to see chough.

Seven raptors occur regularly on Colonsay and Oronsay with the common buzzard being the most numerous. Kestrel numbers have declined, perhaps as a result of competition with buzzards for nesting sites. Sparrowhawks can be seen anywhere on the islands and there's a good chance of seeing peregrines around the cliffs of Colonsay's west coast. Merlins and hen harriers can be seen, although neither has nested on the islands in recent years. There is one nesting pair of golden eagles on Colonsay, though they have not bred in over a decade. The osprey and sea eagle (or white-tailed) are occasionally spotted.

There are 14 species of seabird breeding on Colonsay. Guillemots are the most numerous with a population of 26,000 recorded on the cliff ledges of the western and northern coast. Kittiwakes, fulmars and razorbills also swell the seabird numbers along the island's high cliffs. The islands have resident populations of Canada geese (about 60) and greylag geese (about 200), and wintering populations of barnacle geese (about 400) and white-fronted geese (about 250). The eider (*lach colonsa*) has long been known as the Colonsay duck. It is possible that the birds arrived on the island along with the Norsemen at the end of the ninth century. Between 100–150 pairs of eider breed on the island each year. Waders such as dunlin, turnstone, sanderling and golden plovers can be seen in small bays around the island with the eastern side of the Ardskenish peninsula and Tràigh nam Barc being especially propitious.

PLANTS AND FLOWERS

Colonsay and Oronsay's mild, damp, almost frost-free climate, plentiful sunshine and fertile soils provide suitable conditions for a wide range of plants, flowers and trees to flourish. On the north-east of Colonsay there are two areas of mixed deciduous woodland at Rubha na Coille Bige and Beinn nam Fitheach reckoned to be one of the finest surviving remnants of native Hebridean woodland anywhere. Here you will find birch, sessile oak, hazel, willow and rowan, which shelter ferns, mosses, lichens and liverworts. In spring the woodland floor is covered with bluebells, violets, primroses and wood sorrel.

The west of the island is susceptible to ferocious salt-laden winds in winter, but the exotic woodland and gardens of Colonsay House at Kiloran are protected by a thick belt of shelter trees. Here you will find magnolia, tree ferns, cordylines and one of the best rhododendron gardens in Scotland. Elsewhere, the west is virtually treeless and the peaty soil sustains a variety of bog plants including heather, bracken, willow and bog myrtle, along with bog asphodel, sundews, mosses and bog cotton.

There are large tracts of coastal machair at Balnahard, Kiloran, Ardskenish, Machrins and Oronsay that erupt into bloom in May, building to a floral crescendo in July. Species include buttercups, bird's foot trefoil, saxifrages and carline thistle, scarlet pimpernel, eyebright, clover, thyme,

Orchids abound at Uragaig in spring and early summer

the island as the postbus service was withdrawn in May 2009. Kevin Byrne runs minibus tours of the island on Tuesdays, by arrangement, and on Wednesdays for day visitors arriving on the Port Askaig ferry: reservations on 01951 200320. Cycling is a good way of getting around the island. Bring your own or hire one from Archie McConnel at Upper Kilchattan, tel 01951 200355.

WHEN TO GO

Colonsay and Oronsay are a wonderful retreat from the world at any time of year, though realistically the winter months are not ideal for walking on account of the ferocious winds that frequently batter in off the Atlantic. This far north-west, the days are also short. Fine weather isn't exceptional during the winter, but planning a walking holiday on Colonsay in January is not advisable.

Spring, summer and autumn are all viable seasons for walking here; May, June and July are often balmy and the island is at its most beautiful during these months, verdant and festooned with flowers. Despite their compact scale, the islands never seem

wild pansy, violets, harebell, daisy, silverweed and hawkbit, mountain everlasting, gentians and orchids. Much of Colonsay and Oronsay seems to be carpeted with orchids in the summer months.

GETTING AROUND

With less than 16km (10 miles) of road on the island, there is little point in bringing a car to Colonsay, especially if walking is the main object of your trip. There is no public transport on crowded even at the height of the season. The perennial midge is the small-winged invertebrate in the ointment during the summer months, however, along with the cleg – a small, aggressive horse fly that hangs around in gangs and delivers a stinging bite to which some people have an adverse reaction.

The weather can be unpredictable in the autumn, but you might expect some good weather over the course of a week. A visit in early September can be timed to coincide with the Colonsay Music Festival, which attracts luminaries from the Scottish folk scene and beyond.

ACCOMMODATION

Serviced accommodation on the island includes the **Colonsay Hotel**, which has a restaurant and bar, tel 01951 200316 or 200312. There are also several bed and breakfasts (see Appendix A).

The **Colonsay Estate** has 25 holiday cottages available to rent on the island. The properties include crofting cottages, farmhouses and former estate houses. Prices vary by property and season. For more information go to www.colonsayestate.co.uk or call Scot Omar on 01951 200312. The Estate also maintains a very well appointed Backpackers Lodge, which is situated between Kiloran and Scalasaig, overlooking Loch Fada. There is a launderette available free to guests at Colonsay House 1km from the lodge.

There are no designated campsites on Colonsay and Oronsay, but **wild camping** is permitted in accordance with the Land Reform (Scotland) Act 2003. However, camping is restricted to areas where access rights are exercisable. The Scottish Outdoor Access Code (see 'Accommodation' in the Jura section) spells out campers' responsibilities, which are only common sense. In addition to these general considerations, it is important to be aware of bird nesting areas when camping on Colonsay and Oronsay.

AMENITIES

Scalasaig is the tiny hub of these miniature islands, catering for most quotidian needs. The **Colonsay General Store**, 200m north-west of the pier, stocks basic supplies and foodstuffs alongside organic produce and 'gourmet' items. Most produce arrives by ferry and fresh produce, such as fruit and vegetables, can disappear from the shelves quickly. However, there is an online order service at www.colonsayshop.net or you can phone in orders on 01951 200266 and collect them on arrival – or have them delivered for a small charge. Attached to the shop is the **Post Office**, which stocks a range of postcards, stationery and other items. It is managed by Keith Rutherford who is up to date with tide tables for making the crossing to Oronsay, tel 01951 200323.

The Pantry is a licensed family restaurant and tearoom situated about 100m from the pier. As well as a range

Scalasaig

of meals, snacks, cakes and hot and cold drinks The Pantry sells locally produced gifts and souvenirs. Bread and cakes are baked to order and reservations can be made for busy periods, such as before an evening ferry, tel 01951 200325. The Pantry is frequented by many islanders and you may hear Gaelic spoken here.

The Service Point, just next to the pier, is open five mornings a week between 9.30am and 12.30pm. You can use the internet here, get your photocopying done, send and receive faxes and even make video conference calls. The **Public Library** is also based here. The **Heritage Centre**, opposite the pier, houses exhibitions of art and crafts. The island's small bookshop at Port Mòr has a large selection of titles specialising in local and pan-Hebridean subject matter. There is an antiquarian and rare books section and craft items, woollen items, cards and small gifts are for sale. The **Colonsay Bookshop** is open in summer, Monday to Saturday, opening 12–5pm on Wednesdays and Saturdays and 2–5 pm on the other days. For further information tel 01951 200232 or email bookshop@ colonsay.org.uk.

WALK 9
South Colonsay coast and Oronsay

Distance	30km (18½ miles)
Time	7–8hrs
Start	Junction of B8086 and B8087 at Scalasaig
	Grid ref: NR941395
Map	OS Explorer 354

This fantastic walk takes in 30km of beautiful coastline with many white sand beaches and wonderful views – in summer pack some swimwear. Much of the walk is on fairly level terrain and there are several route variations available. However, forward planning is necessary as access to Oronsay across the sand flats of The Strand is subject to the tide. The period when the crossing can be made varies between one and three hours either side of low tide. Ask Keith Rutherford at the Colonsay Post Office for the latest tide tables or purchase tide tables from Nancy Black of Oban, tel 01631 562550. Oronsay is an RSPB nature reserve so dogs must be kept on a lead at all times.

At the road junction in Scalasaig, follow the signs for The Pantry café. Pass in front of the café and go through a metal gate. Turn left up a slight incline behind the café and follow the vague path cutting across the point of **Rubha Dubh**. Head towards the shore south of Rubha Dubh, but keep to the ground above the rocky coastline as you continue south-west towards a small sandy bay – keep an eye open for seals and otters. Cross the beach and at the far side step up onto some rocks, then clamber through a livestock fence and up the slope onto level ground. The going can be a bit boggy for the next 1km or so with the additional aggravation of dense bracken, heather and myrtle.

Continue on around **Rubha Eilean Mhàrtain**, through intermittently rocky terrain, then pass inside a long dry-stone wall just above the shore before arriving at another sandy beach. Pass through a gateway after 100m or so and cross the beach before clambering over bracken-covered rocks around **Rubha Dubh**. Carry on round to Port a' Chrochaire. Pass inside a livestock fence there and follow it for a few hundred metres, exiting through a rusty metal gate. Pass around or cross the sandy inlet at Port na Bèiste, subject to the tide, and climb up and over the sand dunes on the far side. Drop down to the beautiful sandy bay at Tràigh an Eacail, which frames splendid views south-east to Islay and Jura. Cross the bay and

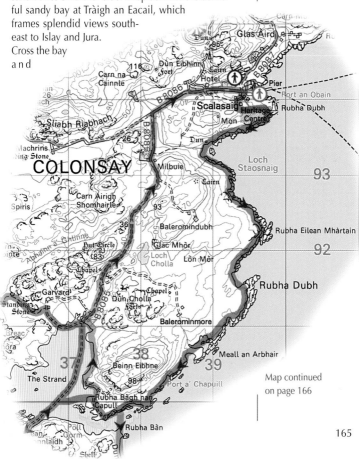

Map continued on page 166

Map continued
on page 170

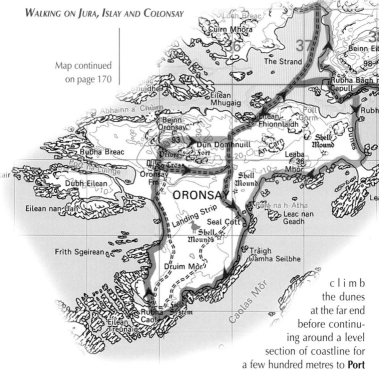

c l i m b
the dunes
at the far end
before continu-
ing around a level
section of coastline for
a few hundred metres to **Port
a' Chapuill**. If the tide is out, walk along
the lovely sandy strand then over an area of dunes
and rocks to emerge at the large bay between Colonsay
and Oronsay.

At low tide, this area is an expanse of sand with only
the serpentine channel winding through the bay prevent-
ing passage across to the dunes on Oronsay's east coast.
However, it is possible to cross to Oronsay at this point if,
with exceptional good fortune or obsessive forward planning, you arrive here to coincide with a spring tide.

If you manage to cross here (marked in blue on the
map), continue along the shore past **Rubha Bàn** and follow the broad, dune-backed sandy beach on Oronsay's
east coast. After several hundred metres, cut across the
promontory at the island's eastern extremity and continue

Chapuill

westwards around the coast. Where the shoreline becomes very rocky, find a route through the rocky outcrops above the shore until you arrive at a sandy bay where the coast turns south again. Continue along the beach for half a kilometre until you arrive at **Seal Cottage**. Here on the eastern side of Oronsay there are a number of conspicuous Mesolithic shell mounds, small hillocks up to 30m in diameter and 3.5m high, dating from around 7000BC (see 'History' section).

At times other than exceptional spring tides, when it is not possible to cross between the islands along the eastern shore, head west across the sandy shore at Colonsay's south-eastern tip and then up and over the promontory of **Rubha Bàgh nan Capull** to arrive on the tidal sand flats of **The Strand**. If you've arranged your walk to coincide with the tidal 'window', follow the tyre tracks that emerge from the shoreline below the houses at **Poll Gorm** and head south-west across the flats to Oronsay. Flip-flops can be useful here. After 500m or so you will pick up a track road that continues south-west, skirting the coast of Oronsay for a further 500m before coming ashore by **Eilean Fhionnlaidh**. Follow the track road for a further 1km as it climbs a little then turns south after 500m. Where the track bends west to follow the course of a dry-stone wall, pass through a gate and head south for several hundred metres, passing through a gateway in a second dry-stone wall, before turning south-east and making for Seal Cottage, which sits amid the dunes above the shore.

Looking across Rubha Ban to Oronsay

Seal Cottage at Oronsay

Seal Cottage is owned by the Oronsay Estate and is really worth a look. Although the cottage is not open to the public, the large, arched, many-paned window to the seaward side allows views into the beautiful sitting room – a maritime fantasia adorned with a scallop shell-framed mirror, glass float and wrought-iron chandelier, whale bones and driftwood.

From Seal Cottage, follow the beautiful, low-lying coastline south-west along or above the sandy shore for about 2km until it turns north from **Rubha Caol**. There is a Landrover track covering the 2km from Rubha Caol to Oronsay Farm and the ruins of the Augustinian priory, but the dunes and beaches along Oronsay's west coast are magnificent and therefore make the better walking route. However, around 1km north of Rubha Caol, a rocky outcrop with a steep drop blocks the shoreline route, so follow a dry-stone wall inland for 200m and pass through the gateway before heading back to the shore.

Make your way along the glorious stretch of dune-backed beach facing the vast Atlantic. Near its northern end follow the right bank of a small burn away from the shore and then follow the track through a gate in a livestock fence. Go through a gateway in a dry-stone wall 200m further on, then pass along a wall-lined track, which emerges onto the main track from The Strand to **Oronsay Farm** 200m further on. Turn left for the farm and the priory ruins.

ORONSAY PRIORY

The surviving ruins of Oronsay's Augustinian monastic priory date from the mid-14th century and it is thought that the priory was founded by John of Islay, Lord of the Isles. However, the site retains traces of an ancient monastic settlement on the site, dating from the sixth century. The existence of an earlier monastic community here links the site to Saint Columba, who is said to have landed on Oronsay on his way from Ireland to Iona – where he established the important ecclesiastical centre that eventually became Iona Abbey. The walled precincts of Oronsay Priory contain the church ruins, the beautiful cloister with its unusual gable arches, a burial ground and an immense, elaborately carved late-medieval stone cross known as the Oronsay Cross or Prior Colin's Cross. The Prior's House is home to around 30 ornate medieval tombstones.

Meall Lamalum

Port Bàn

139

Beinn Bhreac

Binnein Riabhach
120

Mullairidh

Tòrr-an

Chapel Sch

Map continued
from page 166

Gortain

Upper Kilchattan

38

An Rubha

Chapel

Standing Stones

Lower Kilchattan

Cemy

Carn Mòr 134

Port Mòr

Eilean nam Ban

Dubh Loch

Dùn Meadhonach

Carn na Cainnle

Raised Beaches

Dùn

Beinn nan 126 Caorach

Rubh' Àird Alanais

Tobar Fuar

12

Sliabh Riabhach

26

Eilean Dubh

Machrins Standing Stone

COLONSAY

Dùn Gallain fort

Airstrip

Carn Airigh Shomhairle

Port Lobh

Carn Spiris

36

Eilean a' Chladaich

Plaide Mhòr

Tùrnigil

Càrn Glas

Carn Chaointe

Abhainn a' Chùinne

Hut Circle (83)

Chapel

Sguide an Lean

Dùnes

Eilean na Bilearach

Ardskenish

Tràigh nam Bàrc

Garvard

Dùn Cho fort

B8085

Dùn

Standing Stone

34 35 36 37 Beinn

Rubh' an Dùnain

Cùirn Mhòra

Loch Breac

Glas Eilean

22

The Strand

Rubha Capull

Sgeirean Fada

Leac Bhuidhe

Eilean Mhugaig

Poll Gorm

Abhainn a' Chùirn

170

Beinn Oronsay

Eilean Fhionnlaidh

Carn

93

Dùn Domhnuill fort

Rubha Breac

Priory

It is worth scaling **Beinn Oronsay**, which looms immediately to the north-east of Oronsay Farm, rising up out of Oronsay's flatlands to 93m in height and affording commanding views south and east to Jura and Islay and north over The Strand to Colonsay. Beinn Oronsay is easily climbed (marked in blue on the map) by setting off up its flank from the main track a couple of hundred metres east of the priory. From the top of the hill, either descend east along its rocky slopes to rejoin the main track – being vigilant for boggy tracts – or simply descend by the route you climbed. Either way, return along the main track to The Strand and cross the 1.5km of sand flats, not the way you came, but north-east towards the southern end of the **B8085**, following the tyre tracks.

Before reaching the parking area at the road end, turn north-west off the main route and make for the track several hundred metres distant that should be visible climbing ashore south-east of Garvard (NR368910). Once on the track, follow it up a slight incline, through a gate in a dry-stone wall and continue on to a junction by a byre or outbuilding. Follow the left hand branch of the track for 1km as it weaves through rocky outcrops and low-lying ground – a ford in the track has become permabog, so you will need to skirt around it. Arriving at the edge of **Tràigh nam Bàrc**, head west across the flat, sandy expanse to the dunes of the **Ardskenish** peninsula on the far side. The tide goes out around 700m between high and low water at Tràigh nam Bàrc; at high tide, follow the shore around to the north-west, though the tide will be low here if you have crossed The Strand.

Once at the far side of Tràigh nam Bàrc, head up into the sand dunes and look for a distinct track that will take you across to their northern extremity above the beautiful beaches of the peninsula's north shore. The track becomes rocky at this point and climbs a little as it bends north-east between rocky hillsides then drops again through boggy ground before turning north. Take the path that peels off the main track to the left and follow it around the beach at **Port Lobh**, crossing a burn and passing by the western end of the perimeter fence around Colonsay's tiny airstrip.

Head across country towards the sandy beach at Tràigh an Tobair Fhuair, taking care to avoid boggy ground en route. Cross the beach and pick up the track that bends to the north-east by the large rusting structure above the shore. Follow the track around to a raised beach and up onto the **B8086**. From here it is 1km to Lower Kilchattan and 5km to Scalasaig.

An alternative route when returning across The Strand is to continue north to the parking area and then return the 5km to **Scalasaig** by road. Simply follow the B8085 north for 3km or so to the junction with the B8086, then turn right and walk the remaining 1.5km to Scalasaig.

Another alternative, if the crossing to Oronsay is not viable, is to continue north around the coast from **Rubha Bàgh nan Capull** to the parking area at the end of the B8085 and pick up the cairn-marked route across the sand flats to the start of the path at NR368910 – and then around the coast to **Lower Kilchattan**. This option can be extended by incorporating the Ardskenish peninsula, which is fairly straightforward to walk around and offers splendid views in all directions. It is possible to stay close to the shore on much of the south-eastern side of the Ardskenish peninsula, though it becomes rockier towards the point, requiring a retreat to higher ground. The off-shore rocks around **Glas Eilean**, south-east of the point, are popular with seals. Keep to the clifftop around the point then along the north-west coast and past **Ardskenish House**, before dropping down to the shore to walk along the beautiful beaches for the last 1km or so, before picking up the track again by **Carn Glas** (NR352923).

White sands on the Ardskenish peninsula

WALK 10
Lower Kilchattan to Kiloran Bay

Distance	To Kiloran Bay 6km (3½ miles); for return by B8086 add 5km (3 miles)
Time	To Kiloran Bay 2½–3hrs; for return by B8086 add 1½hrs
Start	B8086 opposite Colonsay Bookshop Grid ref: NR362948
Map	OS Explorer 354

This section of Colonsay's west coast can be walked as an out and return route or as part of a longer circular route from Lower Kilchattan to Scalasaig around the north of the island via Kiloran Bay and Balnahard Bay by adding it to Walk 11. Much of this walk is along or near high cliffs and care should be exercised at all times and especially in windy conditions.

From the B8086, take the track heading north-east opposite the Colonsay Bookshop (NR362948). After 100m you will arrive at a gate; don't go through it but follow the fence towards the shore and pass around it. From here follow the vague path around the shore on the outside of the fence until you come to a step stile over the fence just past a gate. Go over and continue on your way, making use of the sheep tracks that forge a route fringing the rocky shore. As you gain a little height, keep to the paths nearest the cliffs and, initially at least, keep to the seaward side of the western

Map continued on page 176

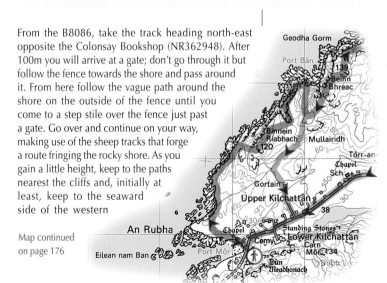

flank of **Binnein Riabhach**, which climbs to 120m and dominates this section of the coast. At times there are good views of the cliff face below and the many sea-birds nesting here, including fulmars, guillemots, razor-bills, cormorants, shags and kittiwakes.

When the clifftop route becomes impassable, find a route up to the summit of Binnein Riabhach; you may have to cross a livestock fence once or twice to do so. There are good 360° views to be had from here (NR364964). Descend north-east on a gentle gradient for around 500m until you arrive at the point of Aoineadh an t-Sruth where you will be looking onto the broad V-shaped gully leading to Meall Lamalum ('lamb's holm promontory'). Head back inland along the edge of the gully until you can safely descend into it, then follow the path on the far side of the gully that soon steers around the coast on the flank of Lamalum, above the sloping promontory of Meall Lamalum and the small bay at Leum a' Bhriair. Continue following the path round, staying high up on the grassy slope, until you can see a way down to Meall Lamalum. ◄

It is worth looking round this promontory as there are good views onto cliffs swarming with sea birds.

Gulls and razorbills nesting at Meall Lamalum

THE ARANDORA STAR

On the clifftop above Leum a' Bhriair there is a cairn and plaque commemorating Giuseppe Delgrosso, whose body was found washed ashore here by islanders during the last war. Delgrosso was an Italian civilian who was among more than 800 victims drowned when the *Arandora Star* was torpedoed by a German U-boat off the coast of Ireland when transporting internees to Canada on 2 July 1940.

There were 1673 passengers and crew aboard the *Arandora Star*, including a 200-man military escort, 479 German internees, 86 German POWs and 734 Italians, many of whom had been resident in Scotland and were rounded up after Italy had allied herself to the Axis powers in June 1940.

The *Arandora Star* set sail for Canada without convoy, dangerously overloaded and with lifeboat capacity for only 500. Furthermore, she was painted battleship grey with no Red Cross or other means of identification, giving her the appearance of a troop carrier – a target no U-boat commander would refuse. Many of those who drowned were caught in an oil slick from the stricken vessel. Survivors were picked up by two Allied destroyers. Some of them were subsequently transported to Australia. The remains of most of those who perished were never recovered, though a small number were eventually washed ashore on Colonsay, including Giuseppe Delgrosso who was buried in the cemetery at Lower Kilchattan.

Continuing around the clifftop from Meall Lamalum, you will soon find yourself above **Port Bàn** and the beach popularly known as Pig's Paradise, which sits beneath the seabird-infested cliffs of Aoineadh nam Muc (or 'terrace of the pigs' – so named because islanders once kept their pigs penned here). A path leads down to the beach, which is worth exploring.

Returning from the beach, head back inland to walk south-west at the foot of a steep escarpment until you can

Map continued
from page 173

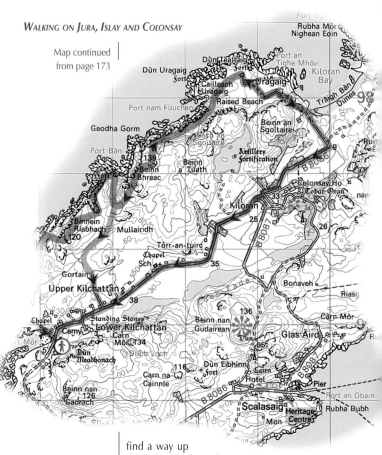

As well as the
abundant seabirds,
peregrines, merlins
and choughs are seen
in this area.

find a way up
the hillside where the
incline is gentler. Look for a path that will take you north-
east to the top of **Beinn Bhreac**. A step-over stile crosses
a long dry-stone wall (NR374968) before you reach the
top. ◄

Descend gently for a few hundred metres along the
clifftop, which can be boggy in places, and when the
ground drops more precipitously look for a vague path
that descends to the left of a burn (NR376974). After dropping perhaps 50m, follow the more or less well-defined

path that weaves its way along the clifftops, giving grand views onto the promontory at Uragaig. After 500m, cross a dry-stone wall and fence (NR383977); find a path on the other side and descend through some rocky outcrops until you arrive on the beach at **Port nam Fliuchan**. This is a fine little bay that makes for good, sheltered swimming in clement conditions.

Port nam Fliuchan at Uragaig

> The western end of the Uragig promontory is worth exploring for the rock arches and the site of the Bronze Age fort at Dùn Uragaig. This area is called **Cailleach Uragaig** – the Old Woman of Uragaig – as the rocky profile of the promontory is said to resemble the prone form of an old hag (when viewed from above the northern end of Kiloran Bay).

Continuing on around the promontory is a bit awkward because of the arrangement of livestock fences along the clifftops. The alternative is to follow the track at the top of the beach (NR384981), which takes you northeast past a couple of houses at **Duntealtaig** before turning south-east and passing through **Uragaig** then north-east again through Creagan, where the track becomes a road.

Kiloran Bay

Half a kilometre down the road you will find the small parking area above the southern end of **Kiloran Bay** and a gate (NR397977) leading down to the beach via a rocky slope. At the bottom of the slope there is an erratic Loch Fyne granite boulder deposited by the retreating glaciers. Kiloran Bay is famed for its sparkling turquoise waters and beautiful broad sandy beach set amid a rocky coastline dominated by Carnan Eoin (Bird Cairn) – Colonsay's highest peak at 143m. The shore is often pounded by wind-driven, white-crested breakers; however, at low tide and in clement conditions it is an excellent beach for swimming and picnicking.

From Kiloran Bay there are a number of options. You can return to Lower Kilchattan by retracing your steps back along the coast or by following the **B8086** south-west for 5km. If you retrace your steps it is possible to pick up a well-defined track above Pig's Paradise that leads south to the road at Lower Kilchattan, passing by **Gortain Cottage** en route. Alternatively you can walk to **Scalasaig** via the grounds of **Colonsay House** along the Old Road (see Walk 12). For the fit and determined it is also possible to continue north around the coast to Balnahard Bay, then south to Scalasaig as described in Walk 11.

WALK 11
Kiloran Bay to Scalasaig around the coast

Distance	19km (12 miles)
Time	6hrs
Start	Small parking area at western end of Kiloran Bay
	Grid ref: NR397977
Map	OS Explorer 354

The terrain encountered on this walk is varied and includes sandy beaches, clifftops, rocky coastline and woodland as well as Colonsay's highest peak. The second half of the walk from Balnahard Bay to Scalasaig along the east coast is tough in places – much more so in summer when route finding is made difficult by bracken cover. The walk is full of natural beauty and wonderful views, with many interesting man-made structures along the way. If you want, you can add the section of coastline from Lower Kilchattan, following the route described in Walk 10.

Walk north-east for 1km along the sublime sweep of sandy beach at Kiloran Bay. At its northern extremity, make for a stile across a low fence (NR404984). From here, either follow the fence to the track road that climbs steeply, bending to the north-west before levelling out or head straight up a damp gully opposite to join the track where it levels out by some overhead power lines (NR406985). Leave the track heading north-east up a grassy slope towards the col between Beinn Bheag and **Carnan Eoin**. You will soon pick up a trodden path intermittently marked with small cairns that winds its way to the summit at 143m.

These cairns on the flank of Carnan Eoin come with a **legend** attached: members of Colonsay's Bell clan engaged a raiding party of Mull MacLeans on Carnan

Eoin, with heavy casualties on both sides. The remaining Bells only arrived on the scene when the fighting was over. From then on they were known as Early Bells and Late Bells. The Early Bells had followed cairns on the western flank, while the Late Bells followed those to the east.

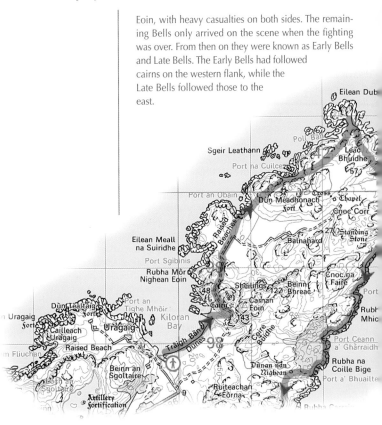

Map continued
on page 183

Atop Carnan Eoin sits a very large stone cairn and this makes for a splendid vantage point from which to enjoy superlative views over Kiloran Bay as well as Islay, Jura and Mull. Looking north-west to Port Sgibinis, 1km distant, you will see the curious Balnahard Whale, a 160m-long pebble 'sculpture', which remains a work in progress and is not easily recognisable at ground level. Much of the whale's front end is formed by a small raised beach appropriated for this purpose. Help to consolidate the whale's tail-end by adding a pebble when you descend.

Return to the track and continue along as it bends north and descends towards **Port Sgibinis** ('ship haven'). Leaving the whale behind, it is possible, though a bit dull, to walk to Balnahard Bay along the remainder of the track road; however, a more interesting option is to continue around the coast. Head north to **Port an Obain**, skirting a livestock fence then dropping down to and crossing the pebble beach (NR409977). Look for a broad gully climbing north-east and head up it, following faint tracks where available. The gully climbs to around 40m before levelling out below the ancient fortified hilltop of **Dun Meadhonach**. Continue along the gully, which soon descends to a boggy area just inland from **Port na Cuilce**, cross a dry-stone wall (NM417002) and follow another gully that climbs gently north-east. The gully soon opens out onto a wide level area that is prone to bogginess; keep to the left-hand side of this area and soon you will be looking down onto **Eilean Dubh** to the north.

Eilean Dubh

Eilean Dubh is not really an island as it is connected to the rest of Colonsay by a narrow isthmus. It is worth following the obvious gully (NM424006) down to the isthmus and exploring the wild, rocky promontory of Eilean Dubh. There is further opportunity to contribute to site-specific artworks as a rather striking structure fashioned from driftwood, flotsam and jetsam is taking shape here.

From Eilean Dubh, head back up the gully, find a route up onto the higher ground to your left and trend south-east without losing any height until you come to a livestock fence. Cross the fence and descend south-east to the machair-like meadow to the rear of **Balnahard Bay**, carpeted with wild flowers in spring and summer. Walk through the dunes and you will arrive on one of the planet's loveliest beaches. ◄ There are fine views across the Firth of Lorn to the west coast of Jura, Scarba, the Garvellachs and Mull. The bay is more sheltered than Kiloran Bay, so between June and September there is no excuse for not taking a dip.

When you finally tear yourself away from Balnahard Bay, walk to its southern end and climb up to a livestock

On a sunny day Balnahard Bay is truly paradise with its expanse of white sand beach and clear turquoise waters.

Beautiful Balnahard Bay at Colonsay's north-eastern tip

fence. Follow the fence west towards the point at **Rubh' a' Geodha** and climb over where it terminates, butted up against a rocky outcrop (NR430998). Once over the fence you are on a very wild section of coast that is very hard work to negotiate in summer on account of the heather and bracken cover. There are goat tracks along this stretch of coast, but they can be hard to follow or even find when the bracken is up. The shoreline as far as Port Araraibhne is largely unnavigable, but don't be tempted to stray too far inland either. As you make your way along to Port Araraibhne you may encounter wild goats.

Once you have reached **Port Araraibhne**

Map continued from page 180

(NR424986) it should be possible to steer a course around the coast for some distance, although this involves negotiating several areas of rocky shoreline and improvising at times. Less than 1km further on you will encounter remnants of deciduous woodland above **Rubha na Coille Bige** including birch, oak, hazel and rowan. Several hundred metres to the south you will arrive at a burn that runs into **Port a' Bhuailtein**; follow it upstream for a couple of hundred metres and you will find the ruins of **Dùnan nan Nighean** ('little fort of the women') atop a rocky hillock (NR416976). Several doorway lintels are still in place and Iron Age pottery has been excavated from the site. The name refers to the MacPhee chiefs' custom of sending their expectant wives to the fort to give birth.

Leaving Dùnan nan Nighean behind, head south past the end of a dry-stone wall and gain a little height, skirting beneath the rocky face of Cnoc Mor Carraig nan Darrach. Descend towards the coast when feasible and you will soon arrive at a second woodland enclosure at **Beinn nam Fitheach** – a surviving remnant of native Hebridean forest. Keep to the seaward side of the enclosure and continue working your way along the coast, passing **Eilean Olmsa** and **Port Olmsa**, where some say Bonnie Prince Charlie first set foot on Scottish soil – though the island of Eriskay also lays claim to that distinction. Half a kilometre or so further on **Riasg Buidhe** ('yellow marsh') will appear a few hundred metres inland (NR406955).

It is worth making the short detour to inspect the ruins of **Riasg Buidhe**. The small settlement was abandoned shortly after the Great War when the residents moved along the coast to Glassard. As well as a graveyard and a scattering of other buildings, a single long terrace of roofless stone-built cottages with vacant window and door frames lends the site an eerie atmosphere.

Return to the coast and pick up a vague path, which arrives at Glassard after less than 1km. Leave the coast and head above the line of houses to reach the **B80807** (NR399948) for the last half a kilometre to Scalasaig.

WALK 12
Scalasaig to Kiloran Bay along the Old Road

Distance	6km (3½ miles)
Time	1½–2hrs each way
Start	Pier in Scalasaig
	Grid ref: NR395941
Map	OS Explorer 354

When combined, Walks 9, 10 and 11 circumnavigate the whole of Colonsay and Oronsay. The following walk is the best route *across* the island from east to west other than by road and follows the course of one of Colonsay's most ancient tracks, known locally as the Old Road. Its length can be extended as an out and return trip or it can be added to Walk 11 to make it a complete circular walk totalling 25km (15½ miles). Alternatively it could be added to Walk 10 in either direction.

From the pier in Scalasaig, head west up the **B8086** arriving at the Colonsay Hotel after half a kilometre. Cross a walled bridge into the hotel's drive, then turn left onto a track road heading to **Scalasaig Farm**, before turning sharply right and climbing steeply towards **Beinn nan Gudairean**.

Map continued on page 186

Perched on a hill to the west of the Old Road, dominating the landscape around, are the ruins of **Dun Eibhinn**, formerly a stronghold of the MacDuffies. Continue on up the track, which is prone to bogginess at times, over the shoulder of Beinn nan

185

Map continued
from page 185

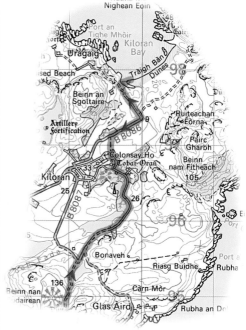

Gudairean and descend the other side, looking out for Tobar na Cailliche ('witches well') to the right of the track at an angle in the fence. The well is equipped with a cup attached by a chain inscribed: 'Wish your will, drink your fill.'

The track descends past Loch Turraman ('murmuring loch') before joining the **B8087** at a sharp bend then leaving it where it bends sharply again after 150m (NR392956). Continue straight ahead where the Old Road resumes as a rough track that soon passes above and east of **Loch Fada** ('long loch') – a body of water that once cut Colonsay in two. The road soon passes through an old gateway into the wooded grounds of the Colonsay Estate, where native species grow alongside exotic sub-tropicals such as acacia, magnolia, eucalyptus and a celebrated collection of rhododendrons. Continue along the

Colonsay House at Kiloran

track past a sawmill and **Avenue Cottage**, before turning right at a junction and continuing on to **Colonsay House**.

Continuing on your way to Kiloran Bay, follow the concrete road that heads north from the small parking area to the east of the house and after a few hundred metres you will join the **B8086**. Turn right and after a several hundred metres turn left along the minor road, arriving at the small parking area above the south-western end of **Kiloran Bay** after half a kilometre.

COLONSAY HOUSE

Colonsay House was built in 1722 and was subsequently added to in the 1780s and around the turn of the last century. The house was built on the site of Kiloran Abbey by the MacNeills, who were lairds of Colonsay until the Strathcona family took ownership of the Colonsay Estate in 1905. The private inner gardens are open to the public on Wednesdays and Fridays and the Garden Café is open on Wednesday and Friday afternoons between 12 and 5pm, serving sandwiches and home-baked cakes. The entrance fee of £2.50 is very reasonable given just how lovely the gardens are. Highlights include a giant yew tree equipped with a swing in front of the house, the ▶

lovely pond with its curious benches and gigantic gunnera plants, and the lighthouse garden, which has as its centrepiece the old lens from Rhuvaal Lighthouse on Islay. Another point of interest is the early Christian statue that stands by a well dedicated to Saint Oran and known as Tobar Oran. The statue dates from the seventh or eighth century and has both Christian and pagan elements. It was removed from the burial ground at Riasg Buidhe on the east coast and brought to Colonsay House in 1870.

APPENDIX A
Accommodation

Looking south to Glengarrisdale Bay

Hotels
The Jura Hotel, Craighouse. Eighteen rooms, dining room and lounge bar serving good fresh food based on local produce, including fresh fish and venison. Camping permitted in hotel garden for a small donation. Shower and laundry facilities for non-residents. Tel 01496 820243

Bunkhouse
Walker's bunkhouse, Kinuachdrachd. Contact Mike and Joan Richardson, tel 07899 912116

Bed and breakfast
8 Woodside, Craighouse. Tel 01496 820319

Kinuachdrachd Farm, North End. Tel 07899 912116

The Manse, Craighouse. Tel 01496 820384

The Whitehouse, Ardfernal. Tel 01496 820393

Self-catering

Boiden Cottage. Located at Ardfernal (6.5km from Craighouse), sleeps up to six. Contact Drew and Christine Fairman, tel 01496 820393

Braeside. Bungalow sleeping five, set above Craighouse. Contact Charles Renwick, tel 0141 946 4361

Heather Cottage. Three bedrooms sleeping up to five at Inverlussa, less than 1km from Ardlussa. Contact Mrs Fletcher, tel 01786 850274

Jura Holiday Let. Three-bedroom house in Craighouse. Contact Kim Henry, tel 01785 614701

Jura House. Can be rented on a weekly basis for groups of up to 15. Contact Mrs Mirjam Cool, tel 01496 820315

ISLAY

Sanaigmore Bay

Hotels

Bridgend Hotel, Bridgend. Tel 01496 810212 or email info@bridgend-hotel.com

Harbour Inn Hotel, Bowmore. Tel 01496 810 3030
or email info@harbour-inn.com

Loch Indaal Hotel, Main Street, Port Charlotte. Tel 01496 850202

Port Charlotte Hotel, Main Street, Port Charlotte. Tel 01496 850360 or email info@portcharlottehotel.co.uk

Bed and breakfast

An Cuan, Jamieson Street, Bowmore. Contact Fergus Muir, tel 01496 810307

Ayen Cottage, Ballygrant. Contact Barry and Carole Jurd, tel 01496 840270 or email bookings@ayencottageislay.co.uk

Caladh Sona, Frederick Crescent, Port Ellen. Contact Hamish and Rhona Scott, tel 01496 302649 or email hamish.scott@lineone.net

Octofad Farm, Port Charlotte. Contact Cathy Wood, tel 01496 850594 or email coultorsay@aol.com

Sornbank, Bridgend. Tel 01496 810544 or email reservations@sornbank.co.uk

The Oystercatcher, Frederick Crescent, Port Ellen. Tel 01496 300409

Tigh-na-Fhothannan, School Street, Bowmore. Contact Mari Johnson, tel 01496 810628 or email mari.johnson@yahoo.co.uk

Self-catering

8 Main Street, Port Charlotte. Three-bedroom terraced house, sleeps six. Contact Les Wilson, tel 0141 946 9037 or email info@selfcaterislay.com

Brae Cottage, Dunlossit Estate, Port Askaig. Three-bedroom cottage sleeps five. Contact Dunlossit Estate, tel 01496 840232 or email office@dunlossitestate.co.uk

Carnain Holiday Cottage, Bridgend. Three-bedroom house, sleeps six. Contact Jan Harper, tel 0131 347 8853

Debbies, Caol Ila. Three-bedroom flat, sleeps five. Contact Debbie MacDougall, tel 01496 850319, email debbie@welcometogreatcoffee.co.uk

Kintra Farm, near Port Ellen. Three cottages with one or two bedrooms, sleeping four to six. Contact Margaret MacTaggart, tel 01496 302051 or email margaretanne@kintrafarm.co.uk

Rhinns Holidays, 83 Main Street, Port Charlotte. Three-bedroom terraced cottage, sleeps six. Contact Linsey Cameron, tel 07890 482815 or email rhinns@rhinns-holidays.co.uk

Campsites

Kintra Farm. Tel 01496 302051 or email margaretanne@kintrafarm.co.uk
Port Mòr. Tel 01496 850411

Cave with view across Loch Tarbert to Beinn Shiantaidh (Walk 1, Day 3)

COLONSAY

Sunset behind Colonsay, viewed from Ruantallain

Hotels
Colonsay Hotel. Restaurant and bar. Tel 01951 200316 or 200312

Bed and breakfast
Corncrake Cottage. Lower Kilchattan. Contact Rhona Robinson, tel 01951 200118

Dharma B&B, Kilchattan. Contact Anne Johnstone, tel 01951 200141

Donmar B&B, Uragaig. Contact Mary MacLeod, tel 01951 200223

Self-catering
4b Glassard. Modern cottage. Contact Mungo Campbell, tel 07956 326 484
5 and 8 'The Byre', Glassard. Modernised cottages, sleep 5 and 3 respectively.
Contact Trevor and Fran Patrick, tel 01951 200354
or email franandtrevor@btinternet.com

Balnahard Farmhouse. Traditional farmhouse, sleeps up to 10. Contact David Hobhouse, tel 07860 763192

Cill a' Rubha or **Longfield**. Modern cottage, sleeps five. Also Phoebe mini-lodge, sleeps three. Contact Kevin or Christa Byrne, tel 01951 200320

Cnoc nam Ban. Traditional crofthouse, sleeps six. Contact Charles or Debbie Jackson, tel 01337 810236

Colnatarun Crofthouse. Self-contained, sleeps up to eight. Contact Archie MacConnell, tel 01951 200355

Colonsay Estate. Twenty-five holiday properties available to rent including crofting cottages, farmhouses and former estate houses. Prices vary by property and season. Contact Scot Omar, tel 01951 200312 or go to www.colonsayestate. co.uk. The Estate also maintains a Backpackers Lodge, between Kiloran and Scalasaig, overlooking Loch Fada.

Craig Mhor. Modern and luxurious cottage, sleeps six. Tel 01620 880282

Craig nan Ubhal. Modern comfortable house, sleeps eight. Tel 01951 200157

Druim Buidhe. Modern cottage, self-contained, sleeps up to eight. Contact Fiona Griffiths, tel 020 8460 6246 or email fgriffkin@tiscali.co.uk

Drumclach Cottage. Self-contained, sleeps up to eight. Contact Pede and Carol MacNeill, tel 01951 200157

Glebe Cottage. Self-contained, sleeps up to four. Contact Rhona Robinson, tel 01951 200118

Island Lodges. Three self-contained chalets, sleep up to six. Contact Ian or Elaine Dawson, tel 01343 890752

Pairc Molach. New house, sleeps up to eight. Contact Jan Binnie, tel 01350 727778

Seaview Croft. Three self-contained cottages. Contact Mrs Annie Lawson, tel 01951 200315

Sgreadan Crofthouse. Self-contained, sleeps seven. Contact Duncan or Margaret McDougall, tel 01951 200304 or 200300

Sunshine Cottage. Self-contained, sleeps eight. Contact Anne Johnstone, tel 01951 200141

Tigh Ur Cottage. Self-contained, sleeps eight. Contact Mrs Libby Fleming, tel 01746 785454

APPENDIX B
Other useful contacts

Sand dunes at Tràigh a' Mhiadair

JURA

Stalking information

If you set out to walk the west coast during the deer stalking season, which runs from 1 July until 15 February, then it is advisable to contact the estates where you will be walking, both for your own safety and as a matter of courtesy.

Barnhill Estate. Tel 01496 820327

Ardlussa Estate. Contact the head keeper, tel 01496 820252

Ruantallain Estate. Contact the head keeper, Craig Rozga, tel 01496 820321

Tarbert Estate. Contact the head keeper, Gordon Muir, tel 01496 820207

Inver Estate. Tel 01496 820223

Forest Estate. Tel 01496 820123

Jura bus service. Operates Monday to Saturday. Contact Alex Dunnachie on 01496 820314 or 820221

Landrover pick-up service from Ardlussa or Road End to Kinuachdrachd. Contact Mike Richardson, tel. 07899 912116

ISLAY
Taxis
There are a number of taxis on the island including:

Carol's Cabs. Tel 01496 302155 or 0777 578215

Rhinns Taxi Hire. Tel 01496 850170 or 0777 1921157

Fiona's Taxis. Tel 01496 302622 or 07808 303200

Lamont's Taxis. Tel 01496 810449 or 07899 756159

Islay Hospital is in Bowmore. Tel 01496 301000

The Police Station is in Bowmore. Tel 01496 810222

COLONSAY
Minibus tours of the island on Tuesdays, by arrangement, and on Wednesdays for day visitors arriving on the Port Askaig ferry. For reservations contact Kevin Byrne, tel 01951 200320

Cycle hire available from Archie McConnel at Upper Kilchattan, tel 01951 200355

APPENDIX C
Glossary

Above the south shore of Loch Tarbert

Gaelic	English
abhainn	river
aird	height, promontory
allt	burn, stream
bàgh	bay
bealach	pass, gorge
beinn	mountain, peak
cladach	beach, shore, coast
cnoc	round hill, knoll
creag	crag, rock, cliff

Gaelic	English
cruach	stack, heap
dubh	black
eilean	island
glas	grey, green
port	port, harbour, ferry
rhubha	promontory, headland, point
traigh	beach
uaimh/uamh	cave

APPENDIX D
Further reading

Raised beach near Shian Bay

Bernard Crick, 'Orwell on Jura', *Spirit of Jura* (Polygon, 2009)

A G Dawson, 'West coast of Jura', *Geological Conservation Review*, Volume 6: Quartenary of Scotland, Chapter 11: Inner Hebrides, 1993

Roger Deakin, *Waterlog* (Chatto and Windus, 1999)

David J Horne, *The Geology of Jura* (DGB Wright, Isle of Jura)

Geological Conservation Review, Volume 28, Coastal Geomorphology of Great Britain, Chapter 6; 'Gravel and 'shingle' beaches'

John Mercer, *Hebridean Islands: Colonsay, Gigha, Jura* (Blackie, 1974)

Roger Redfern, *Walking in the Hebrides* (Cicerone, 1998)

Gordon Wright, *Jura: A Guide for Walkers* (DGB Wright, Isle of Jura)

Peter Youngson, *Jura: Island of Deer* (Birlinn, 2001)

NOTES

NOTES

NOTES

NOTES

LISTING OF CICERONE GUIDES

BRITISH ISLES CHALLENGES, COLLECTIONS AND ACTIVITIES
The End to End Trail
The Mountains of England and Wales
Vol 1: Wales
Vol 2: England
The National Trails
The Relative Hills of Britain
The Ridges of England, Wales and Ireland
The UK Trailwalker's Handbook
Three Peaks, Ten Tors

NORTHERN ENGLAND TRAILS
A Northern Coast to Coast Walk
Backpacker's Britain: Northern England
Hadrian's Wall Path
The Dales Way
The Pennine Way
The Spirit of Hadrian's Wall

LAKE DISTRICT
An Atlas of the English Lakes
Coniston Copper Mines
Great Mountain Days in the Lake District
Lake District Winter Climbs
Roads and Tracks of the Lake District
Rocky Rambler's Wild Walks
Scrambles in the Lake District
North
South
Short Walks in Lakeland
Book 1: South Lakeland
Book 2: North Lakeland
Book 3: West Lakeland
The Central Fells
The Cumbria Coastal Way
The Cumbria Way and the Allerdale Ramble
The Lake District Anglers' Guide
The Mid-Western Fells
The Near Eastern Fells
The Southern Fells
The Tarns of Lakeland
Vol 1: West
Vol 2: East
Tour of the Lake District

NORTH WEST ENGLAND AND THE ISLE OF MAN
A Walker's Guide to the Lancaster Canal
Historic Walks in Cheshire
Isle of Man Coastal Path
The Isle of Man
The Ribble Way
Walking in Lancashire
Walking in the Forest of Bowland and Pendle
Walking on the West Pennine Moors
Walks in Lancashire Witch Country
Walks in Ribble Country
Walks in Silverdale and Arnside
Walks in The Forest of Bowland

NORTH EAST ENGLAND, YORKSHIRE DALES AND PENNINES
A Canoeist's Guide to the North East
Historic Walks in North Yorkshire
South Pennine Walks
The Cleveland Way and the Yorkshire Wolds Way
The North York Moors
The Reivers Way
The Teesdale Way
The Yorkshire Dales Angler's Guide
The Yorkshire Dales:
North and East
South and West
Walking in County Durham
Walking in Northumberland
Walking in the North Pennines
Walking in the Wolds
Walks in Dales Country
Walks in the Yorkshire Dales
Walks on the North York Moors
Books 1 & 2

DERBYSHIRE, PEAK DISTRICT AND MIDLANDS
High Peak Walks
Historic Walks in Derbyshire
The Star Family Walks
Walking in Derbyshire
White Peak Walks:
The Northern Dales
The Southern Dales

SOUTHERN ENGLAND
A Walker's Guide to the Isle of Wight
London: The Definitive Walking Guide
The Cotswold Way
The Greater Ridgeway
The Lea Valley Walk
The North Downs Way
The South Downs Way
The South West Coast Path
The Thames Path
Walking in Bedfordshire
Walking in Berkshire
Walking in Buckinghamshire
Walking in Kent
Walking in Sussex
Walking in the Isles of Scilly
Walking in the Thames Valley
Walking on Dartmoor

WALES AND WELSH BORDERS
Backpacker's Britain: Wales
Glyndwr's Way
Great Mountain Days in Snowdonia
Hillwalking in Snowdonia
Hillwalking in Wales
Vols 1 & 2
Offa's Dyke Path
Ridges of Snowdonia
Scrambles in Snowdonia
The Ascent of Snowdon

The Lleyn Peninsula Coastal Path
The Pembrokeshire Coastal Path
The Shropshire Hills
The Spirit Paths of Wales
Walking in Pembrokeshire
Walking on the Brecon Beacons
Welsh Winter Climbs

SCOTLAND
Backpacker's Britain:
Central and Southern Scottish Highlands
Northern Scotland
Ben Nevis and Glen Coe
Border Pubs and Inns
North to the Cape
Scotland's Best Mountains
Scotland's Far West
Scotland's Mountain Ridges
Scrambles in Lochaber
The Border Country
The Central Highlands
The Great Glen Way
The Isle of Skye
The Pentland Hills: A Walker's Guide
The Scottish Glens
2 The Atholl Glens
3 The Glens of Rannoch
4 The Glens of Trossach
5 The Glens of Argyll
6 The Great Glen
The Southern Upland Way
The West Highland Way
Walking in Scotland's Far North
Walking in the Cairngorms
Walking in the Hebrides
Walking in the Ochils, Campsie Fells and Lomond Hills
Walking in Torridon
Walking Loch Lomond and the Trossachs
Walking on Harris and Lewis
Walking on Jura, Islay and Colonsay
Walking on the Isle of Arran
Walking on the Orkney and Shetland Isles
Walking the Galloway Hills
Walking the Lowther Hills
Walking the Munros
Vol 1: Southern, Central and Western Highlands
Vol 2: Northern Highlands and the Cairngorms
Winter Climbs – Ben Nevis and Glencoe
Winter Climbs in the Cairngorms

UK CYCLING
Border Country Cycle Routes
Lands End to John O'Groats Cycle Guide
Rural Rides No 2: East Surrey
South Lakeland Cycle Rides
The Lancashire Cycleway

ALPS – CROSS BORDER ROUTES
100 Hut Walks in the Alps
Across the Eastern Alps: E5
Alpine Points of View
Alpine Ski Mountaineering
    Vol 1: Western Alps
    Vol 2: Central and Eastern Alps
Chamonix to Zermatt
Snowshoeing
Tour of Mont Blanc
Tour of Monte Rosa
Tour of the Matterhorn
Walking in the Alps
Walks and Treks in the Maritime Alps

FRANCE
Écrins National Park
GR20: Corsica
Mont Blanc Walks
The Cathar Way
The GR5 Trail
The Robert Louis Stevenson Trail
Tour of the Oisans: The GR54
Tour of the Queyras
Tour of the Vanoise
Trekking in the Vosges and Jura
Vanoise Ski Touring
Walking in Provence
Walking in the Cathar Region
Walking in the Cevennes
Walking in the Dordogne
Walking in the Haute Savoie
    North
    South
Walking in the Languedoc
Walking in the Tarentaise &
    Beaufortain Alps
Walking on Corsica
Walking the French Gorges
Walks in Volcano Country

**PYRENEES AND FRANCE/SPAIN
CROSS-BORDER ROUTES**
Rock Climbs In The Pyrenees
The GR10 Trail
The Mountains of Andorra
The Pyrenean Haute Route
The Way of St James
    France
    Spain
Through the Spanish Pyrenees: GR11
Walks and Climbs in the Pyrenees

SPAIN & PORTUGAL
Costa Blanca Walks
    Vol 1: West
    Vol 2: East
The Mountains of Central Spain
Trekking through Mallorca
Via de la Plata
Walking in Madeira
Walking in Mallorca
Walking in the Algarve
Walking in the Canary Islands:
    Vol 2: East
Walking in the Cordillera Cantabrica
Walking in the Sierra Nevada
Walking the GR7 in Andalucia
Walks and Climbs in the Picos de
    Europa

SWITZERLAND
Alpine Pass Route
Central Switzerland
The Bernese Alps
Tour of the Jungfrau Region
Walking in the Valais
Walking in Ticino
Walks in the Engadine

GERMANY
Germany's Romantic Road
King Ludwig Way
Walking in the Bavarian Alps
Walking in the Harz Mountains
Walking in the Salzkammergut
Walking the River Rhine Trail

EASTERN EUROPE
The High Tatras
The Mountains of Romania
Walking in Bulgaria's National Parks
Walking in Hungary

SCANDINAVIA
Walking in Norway

**SLOVENIA, CROATIA AND
MONTENEGRO**
The Julian Alps of Slovenia
The Mountains of Montenegro
Trekking in Slovenia
Walking in Croatia

ITALY
Central Apennines of Italy
Gran Paradiso
Italian Rock
Italy's Sibillini National Park
Shorter Walks in the Dolomites
Through the Italian Alps
Trekking in the Apennines
Treks in the Dolomites
Via Ferratas of the Italian Dolomites:
    Vols 1 & 2
Walking in Sicily
Walking in the Central Italian Alps
Walking in the Dolomites
Walking in Tuscany
Walking on the Amalfi Coast

MEDITERRANEAN
Jordan – Walks, Treks, Caves,
    Climbs and Canyons
The Ala Dag
The High Mountains of Crete
The Mountains of Greece
Treks & Climbs in Wadi Rum, Jordan
Walking in Malta
Western Crete

HIMALAYA
Annapurna: A Trekker's Guide
Bhutan
Everest: A Trekker's Guide
Garhwal & Kumaon: A Trekker's and
    Visitor's Guide
Kangchenjunga: A Trekker's Guide
Langtang with Gosainkund &
    Helambu: A Trekker's Guide
Manaslu: A Trekker's Guide
The Mount Kailash Trek

NORTH AMERICA
British Columbia
The Grand Canyon

SOUTH AMERICA
Aconcagua and the Southern Andes

AFRICA
Climbing in the Moroccan Anti-Atlas
Kilimanjaro: A Complete Trekker's
    Guide
Trekking in the Atlas Mountains
Walking in the Drakensberg

IRELAND
Irish Coastal Walks
The Irish Coast To Coast Walk
The Mountains of Ireland

EUROPEAN CYCLING
Cycle Touring in France
Cycle Touring in Ireland
Cycle Touring in Spain
Cycle Touring in Switzerland
Cycling in the French Alps
Cycling the Canal du Midi
Cycling the River Loire
The Danube Cycleway
The Grand Traverse of the Massif
    Central
The Way of St James

**INTERNATIONAL CHALLENGES,
COLLECTIONS AND ACTIVITIES**
Canyoning
Europe's High Points

AUSTRIA
Klettersteig – Scrambles in the
    Northern Limestone Alps
Trekking in Austria's Hohe Tauern
Trekking in the Stubai Alps
Trekking in the Zillertal Alps
Walking in Austria

TECHNIQUES
Indoor Climbing
Map and Compass
Mountain Weather
Moveable Feasts
Outdoor Photography
Rock Climbing
Snow and Ice Techniques
Sport Climbing
The Book of the Bivvy
The Hillwalker's Guide to
    Mountaineering
The Hillwalker's Manual

MINI GUIDES
Avalanche!
Navigating with a GPS
Navigation
Pocket First Aid and Wilderness
    Medicine
Snow

For full and up-to-date information
on our ever-expanding list of guides,
please visit our website:
www.cicerone.co.uk.

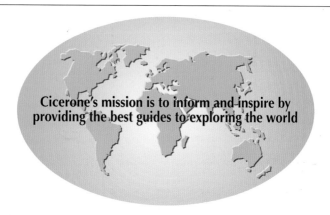

Cicerone's mission is to inform and inspire by providing the best guides to exploring the world

Since its foundation 40 years ago, Cicerone has specialised in publishing guidebooks and has built a reputation for quality and reliability. It now publishes nearly 300 guides to the major destinations for outdoor enthusiasts, including Europe, UK and the rest of the world.

Written by leading and committed specialists, Cicerone guides are recognised as the most authoritative. They are full of information, maps and illustrations so that the user can plan and complete a successful and safe trip or expedition – be it a long face climb, a walk over Lakeland fells, an alpine cycling tour, a Himalayan trek or a ramble in the countryside.

With a thorough introduction to assist planning, clear diagrams, maps and colour photographs to illustrate the terrain and route, and accurate and detailed text, Cicerone guides are designed for ease of use and access to the information.

If the facts on the ground change, or there is any aspect of a guide that you think we can improve, we are always delighted to hear from you.

Cicerone Press
2 Police Square Milnthorpe Cumbria LA7 7PY
Tel: 015395 62069 Fax: 015395 63417
info@cicerone.co.uk www.cicerone.co.uk